Formulas In The Scripture E =MC²

THE KEY TO OUR PENTECOST EXPERIENCE

BY
Lorenzo Hill

Scripture quotations taken from the Amplified® Bible (AMP), Copyright © 2015 by The Lockman Foundation
Used by permission. www.Lockman.org

Scripture quotations taken from the Amplified® Bible (AMPC), Copyright © 1954, 1958, 1962, 1964, 1965, 1987 by The Lockman Foundation
Used by permission. www.Lockman.org

Book Layout ©2017 BookDesignTemplates.com

Formulas In The Scripture E =MC^2/ Lorenzo Hill. —1st ed. Revision 1
ISBN **13: 978-0-9995992-0-4**

Contents

This book is dedicated to Our Lord and Savior Jesus the Christ of Nazareth

67 Then said Jesus unto the twelve, Will ye also go away?
68 Then Simon Peter answered him, Lord, to whom shall we go? thou hast the words of eternal life.
69 And we believe and are sure that thou art that Christ, the Son of the living God.

.

— John 6:67-69 King James Version (KJV)

CHAPTER 1

Eternal Life

Some time ago (I can't recall how many years ago) while out jogging and thinking about the world around me, the Lord provided me with some insight. Knowing that He endowed me with a technical mind, He pointed me to Albert Einstein's equation:

$$E = MC^2$$

Most of us learned this in school when were introduced to Einstein's mental acuity. He was heralded as one of the greatest minds who ever lived. In physics, I learned to interpret this equation to be explained as the basis of the theory that Energy (the E in the equation) can be neither created nor destroyed; it can only take a different form. Therefore, God allowed me to understand that He provided the ability that Einstein possessed and that his work could be expressed in spiritual terms. This is when He gave me His interpretation of Einstein's equation. You have all heard the scientific interpretation of this equation, which is:

Energy = Mass times Acceleration (Acceleration is Velocity Squared)

The Lord gave me another way to interpret this equation. He told me that the initials could be explained this way. In scientific terms, the E in the equation represents Energy. The Lord told me in spiritual terms it represents Eternal Life.

In scientific terms, the M in the equation represents Mass. The Lord told me in spiritual terms the M in the equation represents Man.

The C^2 can be explained in scientific terms as the velocity (or the speed of light) squared. In math, a squared entity can be expressed as that item multiplied times itself. Therefore, another way to express C^2 can be represented as velocity multiplied by velocity or C X C.

The Lord told me this. In spiritual terms, the velocity terms can be interpreted as two individual entities. The first C is representative of Christ. The second C is representative of The Comforter or the Holy Spirit. Therefore, in spiritual terms the equation is:

$$\text{Eternal life} = \text{Man X } C^2 \text{ (Christ times Comforter)}$$

Jesus the Christ came to bring to pass the immortality and eternal life of man and this was the main reason Jesus came to earth. Man, in and of himself is not able to accomplish this task. So, God has made provision through Jesus Christ and the Holy Spirit for this task to be accomplished. Therefore, in spiritual terms, the equation states that man through Jesus the Christ's sacrificial offering for our sin, we can now achieve a similar relationship in spiritual terms as in Einstein's secular work. When man repents and accepts Jesus the Christ as savior and man receives the gift of the Comforter (the Holy Spirit) it results in him receiving Eternal life. Thus, $E = MxC^2$.

Without the sacrifice of Jesus the Christ, who showed us God in human form, we cannot obtain eternal life. The Holy Spirit the Comforter, who teaches us how to be like Jesus, provides the power for this transformation to occur. Without this plan, man was forever displaced from the presence of God.

1 John 5:13-14 King James Version (KJV) (all biblical quotes were copied from the Biblegateway.com site)
[13] These things have I written unto you that believe on the name of the Son of God; that ye may know that ye have eternal life and that ye may believe on the name of the Son of God.
[14] And this is the confidence that we have in him, that, if we ask any thing according to his will, he heareth us:
John 3:16-18 King James Version (KJV)

[16] For God so loved the world, that he gave his only begotten Son, that whosoever believeth in him should not perish, but have everlasting life.
[17] For God sent not his Son into the world to condemn the world; but that the world through him might be saved.

[18] He that believeth on him is not condemned: but he that believeth not is condemned already, because he hath not believed in the name of the only begotten Son of God.

In the scripture, God said man is created in his image. Jesus explained that we receive forgiveness through His sacrifice on the cross and that He left the Holy Spirit the Comforter. He is our teacher and guide to transform us through his teaching to be like Him, to be what God created us to be in the beginning which sin prevents us from obtaining.

Genesis 1:26-28 King James Version (KJV)

[26] And God said, Let us make man in our image, after our likeness: and let them have dominion over the fish of the sea and over the fowl of the air and over the cattle and over all the earth and over every creeping thing that creepeth upon the earth.

[27] So God created man in his own image, in the image of God created he him; male and female created he them.

[28] And God blessed them and God said unto them, Be fruitful and multiply and replenish the earth and subdue it: and have dominion over the fish of the sea and over the fowl of the air and over every living thing that moveth upon the earth.

Colossians 3:9-11 King James Version (KJV)

[9] Lie not one to another, seeing that ye have put off the old man with his deeds;

[10] And have put on the new man, which is renewed in knowledge after the image of him that created him:

[11] Where there is neither Greek nor Jew, circumcision nor uncircumcision, Barbarian, Scythian, bond nor free: but Christ is all and in all.

The change in our image can only can be empowered through the work of the Holy Spirit and the redemptive work of Jesus Christ. This creates in us the ability to be righteous and holy. We need this transformation so that we can enter into God's presence because we cannot dwell in heaven in a sinful state. That's why Jesus had to go to the middle heaven (paradise) to teach those held in the holding place until they could be made righteous.

1 Peter 3:18-22King James Version (KJV)

[18] For Christ also hath once suffered for sins, the just for the unjust, that he might bring us to God, being put to death in the flesh, but quickened by the Spirit:

[19] By which also he went and preached unto the spirits in prison;

[20] Which sometime were disobedient, when once the longsuffering of God waited in the days of Noah, while the ark was a preparing, wherein few, that is, eight souls were saved by water.

[21] The like figure whereunto even baptism doth also now save us (not the putting away of the filth of the flesh, but the answer of a good conscience toward God,) by the resurrection of Jesus Christ:
[22] Who is gone into heaven and is on the right hand of God; angels and authorities and powers being made subject unto him.

Therefore, for man to achieve eternal life, he has to repent and accept the forgiveness provided by the shed blood of Christ Jesus. Then God will provide him the Holy Spirit that has the power to change us into the image that God originally intended for us to possess.

John 17:3 King James Version (KJV)
3 And this is life eternal, that they might know thee the only true God and Jesus Christ, whom thou hast sent.

Scripture expresses these principles more thoroughly than I do. So please read the ones listed below.

Scripture References

Matthew 7:13-14 King James Version (KJV)
[13] Enter ye in at the strait gate: for wide is the gate and broad is the way, that leadeth to destruction and many there be which go in thereat:
[14] Because strait is the gate and narrow is the way, which leadeth unto life and few there be that find it.

Romans 6:23 King James Version (KJV)
[23] For the wages of sin is death; but the gift of God is eternal life through Jesus Christ our Lord.

Matthew 25:46 King James Version (KJV)
[46] And these shall go away into everlasting punishment: but the righteous into life eternal.

John 6:50-71 King James Version (KJV)
[50] This is the bread which cometh down from heaven, that a man may eat thereof and not die.
[51] I am the living bread which came down from heaven: if any man eat of this bread, he shall live for ever: and the bread that I will give is my flesh, which I will give for the life of the world.
[52] The Jews therefore strove among themselves, saying, How can this man give us his flesh to eat?
[53] Then Jesus said unto them, Verily, verily, I say unto you, Except ye eat the flesh of the Son of man and drink his blood, ye have no life in you.
[54] Whoso eateth my flesh and drinketh my blood, hath eternal life; and I will raise him up at the last day.

[55] For my flesh is meat indeed and my blood is drink indeed.

[56] He that eateth my flesh and drinketh my blood, dwelleth in me and I in him.

[57] As the living Father hath sent me and I live by the Father: so he that eateth me, even he shall live by me.

[58] This is that bread which came down from heaven: not as your fathers did eat manna and are dead: he that eateth of this bread shall live for ever.

[59] These things said he in the synagogue, as he taught in Capernaum.

[60] Many therefore of his disciples, when they had heard this, said, This is an hard saying; who can hear it?

[61] When Jesus knew in himself that his disciples murmured at it, he said unto them, Doth this offend you?

[62] What and if ye shall see the Son of man ascend up where he was before?

[63] It is the spirit that quickeneth; the flesh profiteth nothing: the words that I speak unto you, they are spirit and they are life.

[64] But there are some of you that believe not. For Jesus knew from the beginning who they were that believed not and who should betray him.

[65] And he said, Therefore said I unto you, that no man can come unto me, except it were given unto him of my Father.

[66] From that time many of his disciples went back and walked no more with him.

[67] Then said Jesus unto the twelve, Will ye also go away?

[68] Then Simon Peter answered him, Lord, to whom shall we go? thou hast the words of eternal life.

[69] And we believe and are sure that thou art that Christ, the Son of the living God.

[70] Jesus answered them, Have not I chosen you twelve and one of you is a devil?

[71] He spake of Judas Iscariot the son of Simon: for he it was that should betray him, being one of the twelve.

Romans 10:13 King James Version (KJV)
[13] For whosoever shall call upon the name of the Lord shall be saved.

Revelation 21:8 King James Version (KJV)
[8] But the fearful and unbelieving and the abominable and murderers and whoremongers and sorcerers and idolaters and all liars, shall have their part in the lake which burneth with fire and brimstone: which is the second death.

Matthew 7:21-23 King James Version (KJV)
[21] Not every one that saith unto me, Lord, Lord, shall enter into the kingdom of heaven; but he that doeth the will of my Father which is in heaven.

[22] Many will say to me in that day, Lord, Lord, have we not prophesied in thy name? and in thy name have cast out devils? and in thy name done many wonderful works?

[23] And then will I profess unto them, I never knew you: depart from me, ye that work iniquity.

Galatians 6:7-8 King James Version (KJV)
[7] Be not deceived; God is not mocked: for whatsoever a man soweth, that shall he also reap.

[8] For he that soweth to his flesh shall of the flesh reap corruption; but he that soweth to the Spirit shall of the Spirit reap life everlasting.

Luke 23:35-43 King James Version (KJV)

[35] And the people stood beholding. And the rulers also with them derided him, saying, He saved others; let him save himself, if he be Christ, the chosen of God.
[36] And the soldiers also mocked him, coming to him and offering him vinegar,
[37] And saying, If thou be the king of the Jews, save thyself.
[38] And a superscription also was written over him in letters of Greek and Latin and Hebrew, This Is The King Of The Jews.
[39] And one of the malefactors which were hanged railed on him, saying, If thou be Christ, save thyself and us.
[40] But the other answering rebuked him, saying, Dost not thou fear God, seeing thou art in the same condemnation?
[41] And we indeed justly; for we receive the due reward of our deeds: but this man hath done nothing amiss.
[42] And he said unto Jesus, Lord, remember me when thou comest into thy kingdom.
[43] And Jesus said unto him, Verily I say unto thee, Today shalt thou be with me in paradise.

1 John 1:9 King James Version (KJV)

[9] If we confess our sins, he is faithful and just to forgive us our sins and to cleanse us from all unrighteousness.

2 Peter 3:9 King James Version (KJV)

9 The Lord is not slack concerning his promise, as some men count slackness; but is longsuffering to us-ward, not willing that any should perish, but that all should come to repentance.

CHAPTER 2

Prayer And Fasting

While attending a service at my wife's cousin's church, (he is a Baptist pastor), he made a statement to me during his sermon. He called me out by name and stated that there is a formula in the scripture he had just read. He had just read in the book of Mark where a man brought his son to Jesus to have a demon cast out of him. Jesus performed this miracle. The man said he had taken his son to Jesus' disciples but Jesus' disciples were unable to cast out these demons. Later the disciples asked Jesus, when they were alone, why they could not do this. Jesus told them that these demons could not be cast without prayer and fasting. I then understood there was a stepwise sequence (formula) involved in the process that we have to perform in order to be prepared for such ministry.

Mark 9:17-29 King James Version (KJV)
[17] And one of the multitude answered and said, Master, I have brought unto thee my son, which hath a dumb spirit;
[18] And wheresoever he taketh him, he teareth him: and he foameth and gnasheth with his teeth and pineth away: and I spake to thy disciples that they should cast him out; and they could not.
[19] He answereth him and saith, O faithless generation, how long shall I be with you? how long shall I suffer you? bring him unto me.
[20] And they brought him unto him: and when he saw him, straightway the spirit tare him; and he fell on the ground and wallowed foaming.
[21] And he asked his father, How long is it ago since this came unto him? And he said, Of a child.
[22] And ofttimes it hath cast him into the fire and into the waters, to destroy him: but if thou canst do any thing, have compassion on us and help us.

[23] Jesus said unto him, If thou canst believe, all things are possible to him that believeth.

[24] And straightway the father of the child cried out and said with tears, Lord, I believe; help thou mine unbelief.

[25] When Jesus saw that the people came running together, he rebuked the foul spirit, saying unto him, Thou dumb and deaf spirit, I charge thee, come out of him and enter no more into him.

[26] And the spirit cried and rent him sore and came out of him: and he was as one dead; insomuch that many said, He is dead.

[27] But Jesus took him by the hand and lifted him up; and he arose.

[28] And when he was come into the house, his disciples asked him privately, Why could not we cast him out?

[29] And he said unto them, This kind can come forth by nothing, but by prayer and fasting.

I understood that the pastor had spoken these words through the gift of the Holy Spirit. At the time, I wondered why the Lord wanted me to know this. I reasoned that maybe this was for me to prepare for a sermon on this subject. The Lord does this for me from time to time.

"The world we have created is a product of our thinking; it cannot be changed without changing our thinking." - Albert Einstein

The quote above details the attitude that human reasoning produces. Man feels that he in and of himself he can attain all things through his own intelligence. We have to come to realize this is not what God has been telling us.

Afterward I continued to meditate on that scripture. Then a couple of weeks later that still small voice of the Lord told me He wanted me to write a book about formulas in the bible. I tried to dismiss this because I have never written a book. I lacked the confidence that I could do it further, I didn't have the will to do it. I don't enjoy writing and I am not a great typist. So, I tried to ignore this instruction.

A week after this experience, at a church retreat, one of the other ministers asked me point blank about the book I was writing. He told me to let him know when it would be ready because he had some publishing contacts. When he said this my heart leaped for joy! At that point, I knew that it was not just my imagination or a misunderstanding of what the Lord had said. The word I had received was indeed what the Lord wanted me to do. I had not told anyone about the experience I had of the Lord telling me to write this book before this encounter. This was indeed confirmation that I had been told to do this by the Lord. Now, even though I had confirmation of what I had been told by the Lord to do, those feelings of joy were quickly replaced by my initial feelings of inadequacy, doubt and plain old unwillingness. I was then reminded by the Holy Spirit that throughout my experience in ministry, the Lord has proven to me that He will not ask you to do something that He would not equip you to do. So, I quit listening to my mind and will and began to follow the Holy Spirit. Therefore, I started out on undertaking this work.

The formula in this discipline is this:

TPF = M X C²

Where:

TPF = True Prayer and Fasting

M = Man

C² = Christ magnified thru the Comforter

Again, the formula E = MC²-is involved in this process. For without the three components on the right side of this equation the discipline of prayer and fasting does not result in the desired outcome.

I had fasted before but never really understood all that was involved in what I was doing. I just knew that the scripture said to do this and this was an established discipline in the church. I had read several books and commentaries on fasting but they did not seem to supply me with anything other than the mechanics. I thought that if you just did without something (my idea of fasting) that this would bring you closer to God because God would see you were serious about being a believer. Now, the Lord has opened my eyes and my heart to this discipline. I now know more is involved than just abstaining from something and making requests. There are many books on prayer and fasting, so I will not approach the physical part of this spiritual discipline. I am instructed to share with you the spiritual implications.

The inspiration I have received on prayer and fasting is that fasting is nothing without some basic principles being involved.

1. Dying to self and humbling yourself by allowing the Holy Spirit to teach you to emulate the character of Jesus while he was in the flesh. In scripture, Jesus said if you have seen Me, you have seen the Father. Therefore, if we allow the Holy Spirit to teach us to emulate the character of Jesus we emulate the character of God.

2. Fasting is about how we live our lives and about that which we believe. It starts with our everyday walk as a Christian.

3. Fasting combined with prayer adds a dimension that prayer alone does not usually obtain.

4. Fasting is abstaining from a vital part of our life to help us turn our attention towards another vital part of our life that is the need to feed our spirit. It is an act which causes us to change our focus from us to God

5. Fasting has to do with every aspect of our lives including our attitudes and the reasons behind the things we do. It is something that begins by us living a Godly life style. No aspect of who we are is separated from fasting.

Isaiah 58:1-14 King James Version (KJV)
[1] Cry aloud, spare not, lift up thy voice like a trumpet and shew my people their transgression and the house of Jacob their sins.
[2] Yet they seek me daily and delight to know my ways, as a nation that did righteousness and forsook not the ordinance of their God: they ask of me the ordinances of justice; they take delight in approaching to God.
[3] Wherefore have we fasted, say they and thou seest not? wherefore have we afflicted our soul and thou takest no knowledge? Behold, in the day of your fast ye find pleasure and exact all your labours.
[4] Behold, ye fast for strife and debate and to smite with the fist of wickedness: ye shall not fast as ye do this day, to make your voice to be heard on high.
[5] Is it such a fast that I have chosen? a day for a man to afflict his soul? is it to bow down his head as a bulrush and to spread sackcloth and ashes under him? wilt thou call this a fast and an acceptable day to the Lord?
[6] Is not this the fast that I have chosen? to loose the bands of wickedness, to undo the heavy burdens and to let the oppressed go free and that ye break every yoke?
[7] Is it not to deal thy bread to the hungry and that thou bring the poor that are cast out to thy house? when thou seest the naked, that thou cover him; and that thou hide not thyself from thine own flesh?

[8] Then shall thy light break forth as the morning and thine health shall spring forth speedily: and thy righteousness shall go before thee; the glory of the Lord shall be thy reward.

[9] Then shalt thou call and the Lord shall answer; thou shalt cry and he shall say, Here I am. If thou take away from the midst of thee the yoke, the putting forth of the finger and speaking vanity;

[10] And if thou draw out thy soul to the hungry and satisfy the afflicted soul; then shall thy light rise in obscurity and thy darkness be as the noon day:

[11] And the Lord shall guide thee continually and satisfy thy soul in drought and make fat thy bones: and thou shalt be like a watered garden and like a spring of water, whose waters fail not.

[12] And they that shall be of thee shall build the old waste places: thou shalt raise up the foundations of many generations; and thou shalt be called, The repairer of the breach, The restorer of paths to dwell in.

[13] If thou turn away thy foot from the sabbath, from doing thy pleasure on my holy day; and call the sabbath a delight, the holy of the Lord, honourable; and shalt honour him, not doing thine own ways, nor finding thine own pleasure, nor speaking thine own words:

[14] Then shalt thou delight thyself in the Lord; and I will cause thee to ride upon the high places of the earth and feed thee with the heritage of Jacob thy father: for the mouth of the Lord hath spoken it.

The way the Father opened my spiritual eyes to this was by bringing to my mind the scripture that states true fasting and prayer is looking after the widows and orphans.

James 1:26-27 King James Version (KJV)

[26] If any man among you seem to be religious and bridleth not his tongue, but deceiveth his own heart, this man's religion is vain.

[27] Pure religion and undefiled before God and the Father is this, To visit the fatherless and widows in their affliction and to keep himself unspotted from the world.

All of a sudden, the Holy Spirit helped me to understand that fasting and prayer was about living our lives the way God intended, especially with regard to how we are to live with each other. Most of the issues we have with prayer and fasting center around the fact that we do not follow the principles God established. Normal problems with prayer and fasting are:

1.   Prayer is not answered because we seek our own selfish wishes for our own gain. It is about us and our selfish desires (me, myself and mine).

11

2. We pray misdirected prayers. A misdirected prayer is about things that God cannot support because these go against God's principles and plans. Our actions and desires naturally go against His ways. This is due to us doing things in accordance with our own will and based on our fleshly desires.

Luke 18:19King James Version (KJV)
[19] And Jesus said unto him, Why callest thou me good? none is good, save one, that is, God.

3. We do things to make us seem holy and to have others look up to us while not living according to God's principles. This is living the life of a hypocrite and self-aggrandizement.

4. Prayer is not answered when the way we live our lives is not in tune with the guidance of the Holy Spirit or with God's righteousness.

As you can see, prayer and fasting should first agree with God's principles and plans. However, to agree with these, we must first know them. The fundamentals are that it should be about establishing God's ways on earth, His kingdom: Here are some fundamentals:

1. Prayer should be focused on bringing to pass God's righteousness, which will lead to holiness on earth. As it is stated in the Lord's Prayer, "Thy will be done on earth as it is in heaven."

Romans 6:18-20 King James Version (KJV)
[18] Being then made free from sin, ye became the servants of righteousness.
[19] I speak after the manner of men because of the infirmity of your flesh: for as ye have yielded your members servants to uncleanness and to iniquity unto iniquity; even so now yield your members servants to righteousness unto holiness.
[20] For when ye were the servants of sin, ye were free from righteousness.

Psalm 106:1-6 King James Version (KJV)
[1] Praise ye the Lord. O give thanks unto the Lord; for he is good: for his mercy endureth for ever.
[2] Who can utter the mighty acts of the Lord? who can shew forth all his praise?
[3] Blessed are they that keep judgment and he that doeth righteousness at all times.
[4] Remember me, O Lord, with the favour that thou bearest unto thy people: O visit me with thy salvation;

⁵ That I may see the good of thy chosen, that I may rejoice in the gladness of thy nation, that I may glory with thine inheritance.
⁶ We have sinned with our fathers, we have committed iniquity, we have done wickedly.

2. What we loose on earth will be loosed in heaven. In heaven, there is only goodness and mercy. No sin can exist there. In heaven, no one does any harm nor is there any malice on His holy mountain.

1 Chronicles 16:21-23 King James Version (KJV)

²¹ He suffered no man to do them wrong: yea, he reproved kings for their sakes,
²² Saying, Touch not mine anointed and do my prophets no harm.
²³ Sing unto the Lord, all the earth; shew forth from day to day his salvation.

3. Understand that God sees to our needs and just wants. Jesus expressed this as our daily bread. If we are obedient to God, God will care for us just as he did the Israelites in the desert.

Luke 12:29-31 King James Version (KJV)

²⁹ And seek not ye what ye shall eat, or what ye shall drink, neither be ye of doubtful mind.
³⁰ For all these things do the nations of the world seek after: and your Father knoweth that ye have need of these things.
³¹ But rather seek ye the kingdom of God; and all these things shall be added unto you.

4. Forgiveness is not just for ourselves but also for others. We have to learn to trust God to provide just punishment to all. We should show the same compassion toward others as God shows toward us. Again, this is in the Lord's Prayer. We are to pray for those who misuse us. Let God be their judge.

5. Prayer should include looking after the needs of our brothers and sisters. If any has need among us, we are to meet those needs according to the amount of provision God has provided us.

6. We are to love one another as God loves us.

7. We are to fight off temptation, selfish wants and desires.

8. We need guidance in what we should pray for. Therefore, we need to Ask God what we should pray for and how to pray. That is why when we pray the Lord has the Holy Spirit intercede.

Romans 8:25-27 King James Version (KJV)
25 But if we hope for that we see not, then do we with patience wait for it.
26 Likewise the Spirit also helpeth our infirmities: for we know not what we should pray for as we ought: but the Spirit itself maketh intercession for us with groanings which cannot be uttered.
27 And he that searcheth the hearts knoweth what is the mind of the Spirit, because he maketh intercession for the saints according to the will of God.

When we pray, we should ask God to open our eyes to our spiritual needs and for the desire for our lives and the entire family of God to be the same as His. We should also ask God to empower us just as Jesus empowered the disciples to heal the sick, the lame, the deaf, the dumb and the blind and to set the captives free. Free from sin.

All the above is summarized by Jesus in His statements when He stated that we should recognize that God is one God, that we are to love Him with our might, mind and strength and that we are to love our neighbors as ourselves.

Mark 12:28-30 King James Version (KJV)
28 And one of the scribes came and having heard them reasoning together and perceiving that he had answered them well, asked him, Which is the first commandment of all?
29 And Jesus answered him, The first of all the commandments is, Hear, O Israel; The Lord our God is one Lord:
30 And thou shalt love the Lord thy God with all thy heart and with all thy soul and with all thy mind and with all thy strength: this is the first commandment.

Jesus also addressed the topic of fasting in the book of John when Jesus was talking to the Samaritan woman at the well. The disciples brought Him food to eat but he refused the food. Then, He made the statement that His meat was to the do the will of He who sent Him. Jesus then continued teaching those in that area. Yes, Jesus fasted more than once. Yes, let your meat also be to do the will of Him who redeemed you from a life of sin.

John 4:33-35 King James Version (KJV)
33 Therefore said the disciples one to another, Hath any man brought him ought to eat?
34 Jesus saith unto them, My meat is to do the will of him that sent me and to finish his work.

14

[35] Say not ye, There are yet four months and then cometh harvest? behold, I say unto you, Lift up your eyes and look on the fields; for they are white already to harvest.

Therefore, prayer and fasting is about allowing the Holy Spirit to change our focus and our character to be as that of God and Christ Jesus. You should recognize that God, Jesus and the Holy Spirit are one. The Holy Spirit is given to impart the necessary teaching and power for us to do things God's way. Remember God has given us free will and He will not violate that.

The spiritual way to fast is to:

- Humble yourself, Recognize that God is ruler and the creator of all things including us.
- Repent, Admit the sin in your life and seek to be obedient to God.
- Deny yourself; Get away from things that can cause your attention to be turned from God. It will serve as a reminder to keep your attention on God.
- Seek to allow the Holy Spirit to bring about the emulation of Jesus Christ's character in your life.
- Seek God's direction, purpose and His presence more fully in your life.

Ezra 8:21-23 King James Version (KJV)

[21] Then I proclaimed a fast there, at the river of Ahava, that we might afflict ourselves before our God, to seek of him a right way for us and for our little ones and for all our substance.
[22] For I was ashamed to require of the king a band of soldiers and horsemen to help us against the enemy in the way: because we had spoken unto the king, saying, The hand of our God is upon all them for good that seek him; but his power and his wrath is against all them that forsake him.
[23] So we fasted and besought our God for this: and he was intreated of us.

Remember God can only honor a fast done in a righteous and holy way. If we are involved in sin, God cannot recognize living outside of His ways (see Isiah 58:1-9 above).

Matthew 4:3-4 King James Version (KJV)

[3] And when the tempter came to him, he said, If thou be the Son of God, command that these stones be made bread.

[4] But he answered and said, It is written, Man shall not live by bread alone, but by every word that proceedeth out of the mouth of God.

BE PREPARED, Satan will attempt to tempt you with things that appeal **to your fleshly desires:**

- Fame
- Fortune
- Lust
- Covetousness
- Power over others
- And
- Consideration of ourselves above all else

Pay attention to the parable of the ten virgins. Five of the virgins purchased oil to fill their lamps and the others decided to go about their everyday lives and wait until later to seek to the regenerative work of the Holy Spirit. When the call came to come from the bridegroom, five were ready and five were not. The five without oil wanted to borrow oil from the five who had gotten their oil, but they could not. Preparation is something we have to do for ourselves.

Matthew 25:1-13 King James Version (KJV)
[1] Then shall the kingdom of heaven be likened unto ten virgins, which took their lamps and went forth to meet the bridegroom.
[2] And five of them were wise and five were foolish.
[3] They that were foolish took their lamps and took no oil with them:
[4] But the wise took oil in their vessels with their lamps.
[5] While the bridegroom tarried, they all slumbered and slept.
[6] And at midnight there was a cry made, Behold, the bridegroom cometh; go ye out to meet him.
[7] Then all those virgins arose and trimmed their lamps.
[8] And the foolish said unto the wise, Give us of your oil; for our lamps are gone out.
[9] But the wise answered, saying, Not so; lest there be not enough for us and you: but go ye rather to them that sell and buy for yourselves.
[10] And while they went to buy, the bridegroom came; and they that were ready went in with him to the marriage: and the door was shut.
[11] Afterward came also the other virgins, saying, Lord, Lord, open to us.
[12] But he answered and said, Verily I say unto you, I know you not.
[13] Watch therefore, for ye know neither the day nor the hour wherein the Son of man cometh.

Now turn your attention to Anna a priestess at the time of Christ. Scripture states that Anna, after only seven years of marriage, served in the temple until she was 84 years old. Her routine was that of fasting and praying night and day. God answered her prayer and she was allowed to enter into her rest, but her prayer was not answered immediately. Just because you fast and pray does not mean you will get an answer tomorrow. Look at Anna. It took until age 84! (Luke 2:36)

SUMMARY

Prayer and fasting is using a vital element in our life to help us focus on allowing our spirit to be fed (built up in accordance with God's desires for us). Without repentance and the power of the Holy Spirit, our prayer and fasting means nothing to God. Jesus fasted himself. He told the devil at the end of His forty days fast that man does not live by bread alone but by every word from the Lord. He expressed in simple terms that just as our bodies are sustained by physical food, our spirits are sustained by spiritual food (the guidance of the Holy Spirit). We need to separate from earthly things and spend time in God's presence. It is not about giving something up, but using something vital in our lives to help steer our attention towards God.

Matthew 4:3-4 King James Version (KJV)
[3] And when the tempter came to him, he said, If thou be the Son of God, command that these stones be made bread.
[4] But he answered and said, It is written, Man shall not live by bread alone, but by every word that proceedeth out of the mouth of God.

Scriptural References:

Leviticus 16:29-34 King James Version (KJV)
[29] And this shall be a statute for ever unto you: that in the seventh month, on the tenth day of the month, ye shall afflict your souls and do no work at all, whether it be one of your own country, or a stranger that sojourneth among you:

[30] For on that day shall the priest make an atonement for you, to cleanse you, that ye may be clean from all your sins before the Lord.

[31] It shall be a sabbath of rest unto you and ye shall afflict your souls, by a statute for ever.

[32] And the priest, whom he shall anoint and whom he shall consecrate to minister in the priest's office in his father's stead, shall make the atonement and shall put on the linen clothes, even the holy garments:

[33] And he shall make an atonement for the holy sanctuary and he shall make an atonement for the tabernacle of the congregation and for the altar and he shall make an atonement for the priests and for all the people of the congregation.

[34] And this shall be an everlasting statute unto you, to make an atonement for the children of Israel for all their sins once a year. And he did as the Lord commanded Moses.

Psalm 35:11-18 King James Version (KJV)

[11] False witnesses did rise up; they laid to my charge things that I knew not.

[12] They rewarded me evil for good to the spoiling of my soul.

[13] But as for me, when they were sick, my clothing was sackcloth: I humbled my soul with fasting; and my prayer returned into mine own bosom.

[14] I behaved myself as though he had been my friend or brother: I bowed down heavily, as one that mourneth for his mother.

[15] But in mine adversity they rejoiced and gathered themselves together: yea, the abjects gathered themselves together against me and I knew it not; they did tear me and ceased not:

[16] With hypocritical mockers in feasts, they gnashed upon me with their teeth.

[17] Lord, how long wilt thou look on? rescue my soul from their destructions, my darling from the lions.

[18] I will give thee thanks in the great congregation: I will praise thee among much people.

Psalm 69:5-15 King James Version (KJV)

[5] O God, thou knowest my foolishness; and my sins are not hid from thee.

[6] Let not them that wait on thee, O Lord God of hosts, be ashamed for my sake: let not those that seek thee be confounded for my sake, O God of Israel.

[7] Because for thy sake I have borne reproach; shame hath covered my face.

[8] I am become a stranger unto my brethren and an alien unto my mother's children.

[9] For the zeal of thine house hath eaten me up; and the reproaches of them that reproached thee are fallen upon me.

[10] When I wept and chastened my soul with fasting, that was to my reproach.

[11] I made sackcloth also my garment; and I became a proverb to them.

[12] They that sit in the gate speak against me; and I was the song of the drunkards.

[13] But as for me, my prayer is unto thee, O Lord, in an acceptable time: O God, in the multitude of thy mercy hear me, in the truth of thy salvation.

[14] Deliver me out of the mire and let me not sink: let me be delivered from them that hate me and out of the deep waters.

[15] Let not the waterflood overflow me, neither let the deep swallow me up and let not the pit shut her mouth upon me.

Matthew 6:11-21 King James Version (KJV)

[11] Give us this day our daily bread.

[12] And forgive us our debts, as we forgive our debtors.

[13] And lead us not into temptation, but deliver us from evil: For thine is the kingdom and the power and the glory, for ever. Amen.

[14] For if ye forgive men their trespasses, your heavenly Father will also forgive you:

[15] But if ye forgive not men their trespasses, neither will your Father forgive your trespasses.

[16] Moreover when ye fast, be not, as the hypocrites, of a sad countenance: for they disfigure their faces, that they may appear unto men to fast. Verily I say unto you, They have their reward.

[17] But thou, when thou fastest, anoint thine head and wash thy face;

[18] That thou appear not unto men to fast, but unto thy Father which is in secret: and thy Father, which seeth in secret, shall reward thee openly.

[19] Lay not up for yourselves treasures upon earth, where moth and rust doth corrupt and where thieves break through and steal:

[20] But lay up for yourselves treasures in heaven, where neither moth nor rust doth corrupt and where thieves do not break through nor steal:

[21] For where your treasure is, there will your heart be also.

Matthew 9:9-38 King James Version (KJV)

[9] And as Jesus passed forth from thence, he saw a man, named Matthew, sitting at the receipt of custom: and he saith unto him, Follow me. And he arose and followed him.

[10] And it came to pass, as Jesus sat at meat in the house, behold, many publicans and sinners came and sat down with him and his disciples.

[11] And when the Pharisees saw it, they said unto his disciples, Why eateth your Master with publicans and sinners?

[12] But when Jesus heard that, he said unto them, They that be whole need not a physician, but they that are sick.

[13] But go ye and learn what that meaneth, I will have mercy and not sacrifice: for I am not come to call the righteous, but sinners to repentance.

[14] Then came to him the disciples of John, saying, Why do we and the Pharisees fast oft, but thy disciples fast not?

[15] And Jesus said unto them, Can the children of the bridechamber mourn, as long as the bridegroom is with them? but the days will come, when the bridegroom shall be taken from them and then shall they fast.

[16] No man putteth a piece of new cloth unto an old garment, for that which is put in to fill it up taketh from the garment and the rent is made worse.

[17] Neither do men put new wine into old bottles: else the bottles break and the wine runneth out and the bottles perish: but they put new wine into new bottles and both are preserved.

[18] While he spake these things unto them, behold, there came a certain ruler and worshipped him, saying, My daughter is even now dead: but come and lay thy hand upon her and she shall live.

[19] And Jesus arose and followed him and so did his disciples.

[20] And, behold, a woman, which was diseased with an issue of blood twelve years, came behind him and touched the hem of his garment:

[21] For she said within herself, If I may but touch his garment, I shall be whole.

[22] But Jesus turned him about and when he saw her, he said, Daughter, be of good comfort; thy faith hath made thee whole. And the woman was made whole from that hour.

[23] And when Jesus came into the ruler's house and saw the minstrels and the people making a noise,

[24] He said unto them, Give place: for the maid is not dead, but sleepeth. And they laughed him to scorn.

[25] But when the people were put forth, he went in and took her by the hand and the maid arose.

[26] And the fame hereof went abroad into all that land.

[27] And when Jesus departed thence, two blind men followed him, crying and saying, Thou son of David, have mercy on us.

[28] And when he was come into the house, the blind men came to him: and Jesus saith unto them, Believe ye that I am able to do this? They said unto him, Yea, Lord.

[29] Then touched he their eyes, saying, According to your faith be it unto you.

[30] And their eyes were opened; and Jesus straitly charged them, saying, See that no man know it.

[31] But they, when they were departed, spread abroad his fame in all that country.

[32] As they went out, behold, they brought to him a dumb man possessed with a devil.

[33] And when the devil was cast out, the dumb spake: and the multitudes marvelled, saying, It was never so seen in Israel.

[34] But the Pharisees said, He casteth out devils through the prince of the devils.

[35] And Jesus went about all the cities and villages, teaching in their synagogues and preaching the gospel of the kingdom and healing every sickness and every disease among the people.

[36] But when he saw the multitudes, he was moved with compassion on them, because they fainted and were scattered abroad, as sheep having no shepherd.

[37] Then saith he unto his disciples, The harvest truly is plenteous, but the labourers are few;

[38] Pray ye therefore the Lord of the harvest, that he will send forth labourers into his harvest.

Acts 12:22-25 King James Version (KJV)

[22] And the people gave a shout, saying, It is the voice of a god and not of a man.

[23] And immediately the angel of the Lord smote him, because he gave not God the glory: and he was eaten of worms and gave up the ghost.

[24] But the word of God grew and multiplied.

[25] And Barnabas and Saul returned from Jerusalem, when they had fulfilled their ministry and took with them John, whose surname was Mark.

Acts 13:1-7 King James Version (KJV)

[1] Now there were in the church that was at Antioch certain prophets and teachers; as Barnabas and Simeon that was called Niger and Lucius of Cyrene and Manaen, which had been brought up with Herod the tetrarch and Saul.

[2] As they ministered to the Lord and fasted, the Holy Ghost said, Separate me Barnabas and Saul for the work whereunto I have called them.

[3] And when they had fasted and prayed and laid their hands on them, they sent them away.

[4] So they, being sent forth by the Holy Ghost, departed unto Seleucia; and from thence they sailed to Cyprus.

[5] And when they were at Salamis, they preached the word of God in the synagogues of the Jews: and they had also John to their minister.

[6] And when they had gone through the isle unto Paphos, they found a certain sorcerer, a false prophet, a Jew, whose name was Barjesus:

[7] Which was with the deputy of the country, Sergius Paulus, a prudent man; who called for Barnabas and Saul and desired to hear the word of God.

Acts 14:18-23 King James Version (KJV)

[18] And with these sayings scarce restrained they the people, that they had not done sacrifice unto them.

[19] And there came thither certain Jews from Antioch and Iconium, who persuaded the people and having stoned Paul, drew him out of the city, supposing he had been dead.

[20] Howbeit, as the disciples stood round about him, he rose up and came into the city: and the next day he departed with Barnabas to Derbe.

[21] And when they had preached the gospel to that city and had taught many, they returned again to Lystra and to Iconium and Antioch,

[22] Confirming the souls of the disciples and exhorting them to continue in the faith and that we must through much tribulation enter into the kingdom of God.

[23] And when they had ordained them elders in every church and had prayed with fasting, they commended them to the Lord, on whom they believed.

1 Samuel 7:1-11 King James Version (KJV)

[1] And the men of Kirjathjearim came and fetched up the ark of the Lord and brought it into the house of Abinadab in the hill and sanctified Eleazar his son to keep the ark of the Lord.

[2] And it came to pass, while the ark abode in Kirjathjearim, that the time was long; for it was twenty years: and all the house of Israel lamented after the Lord.

[3] And Samuel spake unto all the house of Israel, saying, If ye do return unto the Lord with all your hearts, then put away the strange gods and Ashtaroth from among you and prepare your hearts unto the Lord and serve him only: and he will deliver you out of the hand of the Philistines.

[4] Then the children of Israel did put away Baalim and Ashtaroth and served the Lord only.

[5] And Samuel said, Gather all Israel to Mizpeh and I will pray for you unto the Lord.

[6] And they gathered together to Mizpeh and drew water and poured it out before the Lord and fasted on that day and said there, We have sinned against the Lord. And Samuel judged the children of Israel in Mizpeh.

[7] And when the Philistines heard that the children of Israel were gathered together to Mizpeh, the lords of the Philistines went up against Israel. And when the children of Israel heard it, they were afraid of the Philistines.

[8] And the children of Israel said to Samuel, Cease not to cry unto the Lord our God for us, that he will save us out of the hand of the Philistines.

[9] And Samuel took a sucking lamb and offered it for a burnt offering wholly unto the Lord: and Samuel cried unto the Lord for Israel; and the Lord heard him.

[10] And as Samuel was offering up the burnt offering, the Philistines drew near to battle against Israel: but the Lord thundered with a great thunder on that day upon the Philistines and discomfited them; and they were smitten before Israel.

[11] And the men of Israel went out of Mizpeh and pursued the Philistines and smote them, until they came under Bethcar.

Psalm 51:1-19 King James Version (KJV)

[1] Have mercy upon me, O God, according to thy lovingkindness: according unto the multitude of thy tender mercies blot out my transgressions.

[2] Wash me throughly from mine iniquity and cleanse me from my sin.

[3] For I acknowledge my transgressions: and my sin is ever before me.

[4] Against thee, thee only, have I sinned and done this evil in thy sight: that thou mightest be justified when thou speakest and be clear when thou judgest.

[5] Behold, I was shapen in iniquity; and in sin did my mother conceive me.

[6] Behold, thou desirest truth in the inward parts: and in the hidden part thou shalt make me to know wisdom.

[7] Purge me with hyssop and I shall be clean: wash me and I shall be whiter than snow.

[8] Make me to hear joy and gladness; that the bones which thou hast broken may rejoice.

[9] Hide thy face from my sins and blot out all mine iniquities.

[10] Create in me a clean heart, O God; and renew a right spirit within me.

[11] Cast me not away from thy presence; and take not thy holy spirit from me.

[12] Restore unto me the joy of thy salvation; and uphold me with thy free spirit.

[13] Then will I teach transgressors thy ways; and sinners shall be converted unto thee.

[14] Deliver me from bloodguiltiness, O God, thou God of my salvation: and my tongue shall sing aloud of thy righteousness.

[15] O Lord, open thou my lips; and my mouth shall shew forth thy praise.

[16] For thou desirest not sacrifice; else would I give it: thou delightest not in burnt offering.

[17] The sacrifices of God are a broken spirit: a broken and a contrite heart, O God, thou wilt not despise.

[18] Do good in thy good pleasure unto Zion: build thou the walls of Jerusalem.

[19] Then shalt thou be pleased with the sacrifices of righteousness, with burnt offering and whole burnt offering: then shall they offer bullocks upon thine altar.

CHAPTER 3

God's Word Is Truth

Mark 4:2-20 King James Version (KJV)

² And he taught them many things by parables and said unto them in his doctrine,

³ Hearken; Behold, there went out a sower to sow:

⁴ And it came to pass, as he sowed, some fell by the way side and the fowls of the air came and devoured it up.

⁵ And some fell on stony ground, where it had not much earth; and immediately it sprang up, because it had no depth of earth:

⁶ But when the sun was up, it was scorched; and because it had no root, it withered away.

⁷ And some fell among thorns and the thorns grew up and choked it and it yielded no fruit.

⁸ And other fell on good ground and did yield fruit that sprang up and increased; and brought forth, some thirty and some sixty and some an hundred.

⁹ And he said unto them, He that hath ears to hear, let him hear.

¹⁰ And when he was alone, they that were about him with the twelve asked of him the parable.

¹¹ And he said unto them, Unto you it is given to know the mystery of the kingdom of God: but unto them that are without, all these things are done in parables:

¹² That seeing they may see and not perceive; and hearing they may hear and not understand; lest at any time they should be converted and their sins should be forgiven them.

¹³ And he said unto them, Know ye not this parable? and how then will ye know all parables?

¹⁴ The sower soweth the word.

¹⁵ And these are they by the way side, where the word is sown; but when they have heard, Satan cometh immediately and taketh away the word that was sown in their hearts.

¹⁶ And these are they likewise which are sown on stony ground; who, when they have heard the word, immediately receive it with gladness;

¹⁷ And have no root in themselves and so endure but for a time: afterward, when affliction or persecution ariseth for the word's sake, immediately they are offended.
¹⁸ And these are they which are sown among thorns; such as hear the word,
¹⁹ And the cares of this world and the deceitfulness of riches and the lusts of other things entering in, choke the word and it becometh unfruitful.
²⁰ And these are they which are sown on good ground; such as hear the word and receive it and bring forth fruit, some thirtyfold, some sixty and some an hundred.

The Word of God is bread for living a righteous life. The formula here is:

$$T = M \times C^2$$

Where:

T = Truth of the Word of God

M = Man

C² = Christ X the Comforter (the Holy Spirit)

While doing my scriptural research for this book the Lord drew my attention to the scripture in Mark chapter 4 verses 2-20. He told me that there was a formula in this scripture. The formula derived from the scripture passage above helps us to understand that God has provided us the key to living a holy life. Scripture is that key. It provides us the insight for a deeper understanding of God if that is our desire. We can use scripture by the power and guidance of the Holy Spirit to get to know God and His ways and understand what sin and Satan are all about. It gives us insights into how when we live a life that is apart from God, we will fail at life's ultimate purpose.

There are three spirits in this world, the Spirit of God, the spirit of man and the spirit of Satan. All of these are outlined in scripture. If we study scripture in the power of man's spirit (our intelligence only) we miss the truth of God all together and all we see are words on a page. Then we are left to our own understanding, which is far from what God is. If we are guided by the spirit of Satan, all we see are a bunch of twisted truths. If the Holy Spirit guides us, we find God's love, His will and His power at work in the life of man.

Isaiah 14:11-13 King James Version (KJV)
[11] Thy pomp is brought down to the grave and the noise of thy viols: the worm is spread under thee and the worms cover thee.
[12] How art thou fallen from heaven, O Lucifer, son of the morning! how art thou cut down to the ground, which didst weaken the nations!
[13] For thou hast said in thine heart, I will ascend into heaven, I will exalt my throne above the stars of God: I will sit also upon the mount of the congregation, in the sides of the north:

Jude 6:6 King James Version (KJV)
[6] And the angels which kept not their first estate, but left their own habitation, he hath reserved in everlasting chains under darkness unto the judgment of the great day.

This life is intended to allow man an opportunity to choose to know and accept God's ways or to reject them. In the Garden of Eden and in the desert during the exodus from Egypt man was ashamed of his choices so he hid from God. The direct communication link with God was lost by man's choice not God's. So God provided a method for man to get to know him in a way that would respect man's choice.

Genesis 3:7-9 King James Version (KJV)
[7] And the eyes of them both were opened and they knew that they were naked; and they sewed fig leaves together and made themselves aprons.
[8] And they heard the voice of the Lord God walking in the garden in the cool of the day: and Adam and his wife hid themselves from the presence of the Lord God amongst the trees of the garden.
[9] And the Lord God called unto Adam and said unto him, Where art thou?

Exodus 20:18-20 King James Version (KJV)
[18] And all the people saw the thunderings and the lightnings and the noise of the trumpet and the mountain smoking: and when the people saw it, they removed and stood afar off.
[19] And they said unto Moses, Speak thou with us and we will hear: but let not God speak with us, lest we die.

Man, has always had a choice that is termed as agency. Agency is man's right to accept or reject God. Scripture tells us even the angels in heaven have this choice. That is how Satan and his following, the fallen angels (now termed demons) came into being. Even the demons know God but they do not accept His ways. They have exercised their agency (free will to accept or reject God).

Luke 4:40-42 King James Version (KJV)

[40] Now when the sun was setting, all they that had any sick with divers diseases brought them unto him; and he laid his hands on every one of them and healed them.

[41] And devils also came out of many, crying out and saying, Thou art Christ the Son of God. And he rebuking them suffered them not to speak: for they knew that he was Christ.

[42] And when it was day, he departed and went into a desert place: and the people sought him and came unto him and stayed him, that he should not depart from them.

The Holy Spirit draws man to God. If man accepts His enticing's, the Holy Spirit starts him on a path to get to know God. This is called spiritual growth. The bible says that Jesus is the Word. So, in order to get to know God we must get to know Jesus the Christ, the Son of God. Scripture tells us that all men have the opportunity to know the True God either by the written word or through His creation. Man satisfies his need for a god, whether this is in the form of an idol or man's own intelligence. Throughout the history of man, he has expressed himself through writings. Some of which are good and some of which are bad. The ones that are good can help us learn of God and Jesus The Christ. The most specific work God has provided for a guide to Him and to Jesus is the scripture.

Please note the word "scripture" in this book refers to those scriptures that testify that Jesus is the son of God.

Christian Scripture provides insights into God's dealings with man. However, the words in and of themselves will not provide the insight required for belief in God. Again, man's choice to believe or not believe comes into play here. When aided by the Holy Spirit, scripture can help lead us to know how God works with man and why man should accept Him. It also shows how man's life suffers without God. Therefore, the equation

$$T = M \times C^2$$

is required for the work of the God to go to completion in man.

The road to eternal life lies in the spirit of Man multiplied by the redemptive work of Jesus the Christ and the Holy Spirit. Part of this path is thorough the word (scripture) inspired by Christ in the life of man. God uses the Word to help man to get him to understand that God is the creator and that He is and always has been involved in the life of man.

Consider this example from scripture. The Ethiopian on his way home from worshipping at Jerusalem was studying scripture but he could not understand it. This demonstrates that we need the enlightenment provided by the Holy Spirit to understand scripture's true purpose and meaning.

Acts 8:26-36 King James Version (KJV)

[26] And the angel of the Lord spake unto Philip, saying, Arise and go toward the south unto the way that goeth down from Jerusalem unto Gaza, which is desert.

[27] And he arose and went: and, behold, a man of Ethiopia, an eunuch of great authority under Candace queen of the Ethiopians, who had the charge of all her treasure and had come to Jerusalem for to worship,

[28] Was returning and sitting in his chariot read Esaias the prophet.

[29] Then the Spirit said unto Philip, Go near and join thyself to this chariot.

[30] And Philip ran thither to him and heard him read the prophet Esaias and said, Understandest thou what thou readest?

[31] And he said, How can I, except some man should guide me? And he desired Philip that he would come up and sit with him.

[32] The place of the scripture which he read was this, He was led as a sheep to the slaughter; and like a lamb dumb before his shearer, so opened he not his mouth:

[33] In his humiliation his judgment was taken away: and who shall declare his generation? for his life is taken from the earth.

[34] And the eunuch answered Philip and said, I pray thee, of whom speaketh the prophet this? of himself, or of some other man?

[35] Then Philip opened his mouth and began at the same scripture and preached unto him Jesus.

[36] And as they went on their way, they came unto a certain water: and the eunuch said, See, here is water; what doth hinder me to be baptized?

Early in the morning, when preparing this chapter, the Lord impressed on me to share how my walk with Him and how my experience with scripture has changed. My experience with scripture started just before I was baptized. Many things happened which kept drawing my attention more and more to consider God in my life. Nevertheless, like many I decided to just put this in its place and not really concentrate on God. I had not attended church on a regular basis since my early teens. My focus was on my career and living to get as much as I could. God had done several miraculous things in my life but that did not really cause me to make my relationship with Him a priority.

I had never completely read or attempted to study scripture until just before my baptism. Just before I accepted God's call to baptism at the ripe old age of 29, He got my attention through the miraculous healing of my youngest daughter. She was 14 months old. She had been severely burned and through the anointing of oil and prayer, she was totally healed in a moment. At that time, I realized it was time to develop a true relationship with God because he had really gotten my attention. I then had this overwhelming desire that I needed to study the scriptures to see what they really were saying. I was led by the Spirit to do this. I then read the scriptures. I read in every spare moment. I read them so absorbedly that it only took me a month to read them. After that I could see I needed to make a commitment to God. I had not ever been baptized up until this time. Therefore, at the age of 29, I did something I had never done. I was baptized.

About a year later, I received the Lord's call to the ministry. After my call to the ministry, I would study the scripture based on my need for a sermon or for a class I was taking or giving. Many times, I would experience episodes where the Holy Spirit would provide a special insight into the meaning of certain portions of the scriptures. As I matured in His service, I would find that there were times when I would have an intense desire to read the scriptures. This would happen to me several times each year. At these times, I would start reading beginning at Genesis until I reached Revelations. Now I am not going to tell you that I would read each word. Most of the time I would skip the lineages and I would speed read. The way I learned to speed read was to focus on the whole line and then scan the words. I did not understand numerous passages. For those that I did not understand I would just gloss over those and just go on to the next one. I got study books and commentaries to assist my learning. However, as I became more and more acquainted with scripture the Holy Spirit would teach me from scripture certain things that I needed to know so that I could share them with others.

Commentaries along with my studies in Latin in high school enhanced my knowledge of biblical times and customs when Jesus was here on earth. The New Testament became even more alive to me because most of the books we used to learn the Latin language in high school were written at the time of the Roman occupation of the nation of Israel. I now realize the Lord has been guiding my steps even before I understood that He was the reason why I have made particular choices in life. Has he been doing this with you? I then noticed that I would gain deeper insight into the meaning of the written words in scripture than just the words themselves suggested. I began to see God's hand in the life of people and the true meaning behind the scenes of the scriptural setting. Scripture was coming more alive to me. Many times, I would discuss the meaning that I had gained by the power of the Holy Spirit that was more than the interpretation of reading the words written on the page. I cannot tell you how often I have been told that I did not understand the meaning of the words and what they were describing. So I would stop and allow the person to believe what they were willing to accept.

To be clear, I am a person who likes to use plain language. I am not interested in trying to use words that the common person cannot understand. So even if the concept is deep, I try to keep my speech simple and straight to the point. However, I have found that unless people are open to the Holy Spirit, their ability to receive truth that is more spiritual is limited. Now I don't know it all but I am open to God's leadings. Just as scripture says, we know in part and prophesy in part but when that which is perfect is come then we will know all truth. I have come to know that the understanding of the scripture depends on each individual's willingness to accept what the scripture has to offer.

1 Corinthians 13:8-13 King James Version (KJV)
[8] Charity never faileth: but whether there be prophecies, they shall fail; whether there be tongues, they shall cease; whether there be knowledge, it shall vanish away.
[9] For we know in part and we prophesy in part.

¹⁰ But when that which is perfect is come, then that which is in part shall be done away.
¹¹ When I was a child, I spake as a child, I understood as a child, I thought as a child: but when I became a man, I put away childish things.
¹² For now we see through a glass, darkly; but then face to face: now I know in part; but then shall I know even as also I am known.
¹³ And now abideth faith, hope, charity, these three; but the greatest of these is charity.

Like a lot of you, I used to read all the popular books that would be on the Christian bestseller list. However, I quit doing this because I found that I as too easily swayed by their interpretations. Many times, this would cause me to be confused about God. This is because I could not always relate the information that their writings were indicating about God and I would get wrapped up in their theories and not God's work. At times, I would become more enamored with the author and his ideologies rather than the goal of learning more about God. This is not to say that they did not have legitimate experiences with God but I found that I would become more of a groupie of them than God.

Some of you may be asking, "Why should I trust the things you're writing?" The answer lies in the leading of the Holy Spirit. If he leads you to continue on, then you have your answer. Many good writers out there have prepared some excellent works. When you find one you will know. All I can say is pray about it. If God gives you the nod, continue on, if not put this book aside. It is not for you.

So now, I only read scientific works, the scripture and commentaries on biblical times. Some of the commentaries I have found can create more doubt than increased faith. I also use different versions of the scripture to enhance my understanding and to aid in others understanding when I deliver a sermon. I have always looked to find specific formulas in the bible, but I was using my own understanding and they did not seem to be there.

My understanding of God is he does things in specific patterns which when duplicated can produce the same results. That is how we have learned to produce the technical formulas we use to perform our engineering work. Consider how we calculated how to place men on the moon and bring them back home. This is how we design all the modern devices that we can't seem to live without. I know God provides keys in scripture, just as he has in the world around us, to the mechanisms by which things work. All scientific principles have been produced by God's inspiration through our study of the creation around us. Engineering has come about by studying the laws God has placed in the universe such as electricity and gravity and on and on. Scripture tells us that every kingdom (or every sphere of creation) has a law or a set of rules it follows. If we are diligent in our study of these, He will allow us to find the rules in each set of processes in the world around us.

George Washington Carver wrote in his memoirs how he depended on God to provide him the steps to create the many inventions he produced. He did not use scientific books only the instruction of the Holy Spirit. By God's guidance, he came up with many inventions. With God's guidance, we too can find the keys to spiritual workings by using the tools of scripture enlightened through the Holy Spirit. God is a God of order not chaos or random direction.

When He described the creation in scripture, we see it followed orderly steps. Each step was dependent on the on the previous step.

One thing I can tell you is that God's workings with me have followed an orderly track.

My summary of my experience is this. After Christ drew me to Him, He placed a need in me to study to learn more of Him. The Holy Spirit would provide intense desires for me to study scripture from time to time. As I responded, God would enhance my understanding and I could relate this to those who had ears to hear.

Many study the words in scripture not to find God but for other reasons so they never achieve the original intent for which the scripture was created.

1 Corinthians 2:10-12 King James Version (KJV)
[10] But God hath revealed them unto us by his Spirit: for the Spirit searcheth all things, yea, the deep things of God.
[11] For what man knoweth the things of a man, save the spirit of man which is in him? even so the things of God knoweth no man, but the Spirit of God.

[12] Now we have received, not the spirit of the world, but the spirit which is of God; that we might know the things that are freely given to us of God.

In scripture, you can find God just as you can in the world around us or miss Him. Many try to explain away God by saying there is no purpose or design in the world in which we live. They say that it all started with the big bang. This is their way of denying God. Nevertheless, if we seek him with real intent and purpose all things will testify of Him and He will manifest Himself to us.

Scripture says many are called but few or chosen. Scripture also states that God's desire is for all to be saved. However, if we resist the call of the Holy Spirit this can never happen. As scripture states, we can choose good or evil. Condemnation comes to man because of his choice not to come to the light, which is Jesus, the Christ. Because man may choose to follow his own choices and live the way he wants (not according to the direction in the word or plan of God), man condemns himself. This is not by God's will but by man's choice to go against the rules that God has put in place. This applies to both the churched and unchurched because man may choose to follow his own choices and live the way he wants (not according to the direction in the word or plan of God). This applies to both the churched and unchurched. There are those who have chosen to call themselves Christians but have chosen not to live the life God has ordained just as those described in scripture.

2 Chronicles 7:13-15 King James Version (KJV)

[13] If I shut up heaven that there be no rain, or if I command the locusts to devour the land, or if I send pestilence among my people;
[14] If my people, which are called by my name, shall humble themselves and pray and seek my face and turn from their wicked ways; then will I hear from heaven and will forgive their sin and will heal their land.
[15] Now mine eyes shall be open and mine ears attent unto the prayer that is made in this place.

Again, I call your attention to the parable of the ten virgins. Jesus used this to show that even in the church the opportunity to adhere to the word could be missed. This is because we choose to live our lives based on priorities other than the goal of building His kingdom.

Matthew 25:1-13 King James Version (KJV)

34

[1] Then shall the kingdom of heaven be likened unto ten virgins, which took their lamps and went forth to meet the bridegroom.

[2] And five of them were wise and five were foolish.

[3] They that were foolish took their lamps and took no oil with them:

[4] But the wise took oil in their vessels with their lamps.

[5] While the bridegroom tarried, they all slumbered and slept.

[6] And at midnight there was a cry made, Behold, the bridegroom cometh; go ye out to meet him.

[7] Then all those virgins arose and trimmed their lamps.

[8] And the foolish said unto the wise, Give us of your oil; for our lamps are gone out.

[9] But the wise answered, saying, Not so; lest there be not enough for us and you: but go ye rather to them that sell and buy for yourselves.

[10] And while they went to buy, the bridegroom came; and they that were ready went in with him to the marriage: and the door was shut.

[11] Afterward came also the other virgins, saying, Lord, Lord, open to us.

[12] But he answered and said, Verily I say unto you, I know you not.

[13] Watch therefore, for ye know neither the day nor the hour wherein the Son of man cometh.

Also, refer to the parable of the sower. It describes how those who have been attracted by the Holy Spirit have various reasons for withdrawing from the invitation to come to receive everlasting life. On the other hand, they have chosen to follow other priorities dictated by their situation in life that draw them away from building the kingdom. We can study scriptures and completely miss their intended purpose. The same way we can study the creation around us and not comprehend the hand of God. This is determined by the spirit we choose to follow which is either the spirit of man, or the spirit of Satan or the Spirit of God. Each one will lead us in a different direction. Many study the words in scripture not to find God, but for other reasons so they never achieve the original intent for which the scripture was created. Many try to explain away God by saying there is no purpose or design in the world in which we live. Many say that no intelligent man needs religion. So, the bible is just superstition. Many try to abuse the scripture by trying to find so-called discrepancies or contradictions. Others try to use what they call "historical evidence" to disprove what God has provided. There will always be those trying to oppose God because of the spirit that drives them. I won't try to get into apologetics. For me I know God is real and there is a spiritual truth in existence.

John 3:6 King James Version (KJV)
[6] That which is born of the flesh is flesh; and that which is born of the Spirit is spirit.

Matthew 7:13-19 King James Version (KJV)
[13] Enter ye in at the strait gate: for wide is the gate and broad is the way, that leadeth to destruction and many there be which go in thereat:
[14] Because strait is the gate and narrow is the way, which leadeth unto life and few there be that find it.
[15] Beware of false prophets, which come to you in sheep's clothing, but inwardly they are ravening wolves.
[16] Ye shall know them by their fruits. Do men gather grapes of thorns, or figs of thistles?
[17] Even so every good tree bringeth forth good fruit; but a corrupt tree bringeth forth evil fruit.
[18] A good tree cannot bring forth evil fruit, neither can a corrupt tree bring forth good fruit.
[19] Every tree that bringeth not forth good fruit is hewn down and cast into the fire.

Study of scripture requires a spiritual element to achieve the purpose for which God intended for it. The words of scripture are more than mere words on a page. They can be living words if we pray for God's guidance as we read and meditate on them. God intended for scripture to help us to understand that He is continually reaching out to bring the immortality and the eternal life of man. With the help of the Holy Spirit, we can learn of Jesus from Genesis to Revelation. All aspects of the gospel are provided for this reason because we need to understand what it takes to be like God so that we can live in His presence in eternity, no sin can continue in His presence. There are many other readers of various religious backgrounds today who may know the scripture by memory yet they miss its true intent and lack understanding of the reasons for which the scripture exists. Every feast, every ritual testifies of Jesus the Christ if you follow the direction of the Holy Spirit. The scripture repeatedly tells of the frailty of man's choices and how he has missed God's call or abused his power. Remember the scripture where two disciples were walking along the road when Jesus appeared to them after His resurrection. Scripture states how Jesus explained the scripture to them. Note these were men who had been sitting under His tutelage for 3 years yet they lacked understanding of the scripture. Just as many, they had been exposed to God's words but missed the point.

Luke 24:12-27 King James Version (KJV)

[12] Then arose Peter and ran unto the sepulchre; and stooping down, he beheld the linen clothes laid by themselves and departed, wondering in himself at that which was come to pass.

[13] And, behold, two of them went that same day to a village called Emmaus, which was from Jerusalem about threescore furlongs.

[14] And they talked together of all these things which had happened.

[15] And it came to pass, that, while they communed together and reasoned, Jesus himself drew near and went with them.

[16] But their eyes were holden that they should not know him.

[17] And he said unto them, What manner of communications are these that ye have one to another, as ye walk and are sad?

[18] And the one of them, whose name was Cleopas, answering said unto him, Art thou only a stranger in Jerusalem and hast not known the things which are come to pass there in these days?

[19] And he said unto them, What things? And they said unto him, Concerning Jesus of Nazareth, which was a prophet mighty in deed and word before God and all the people:

[20] And how the chief priests and our rulers delivered him to be condemned to death and have crucified him.

[21] But we trusted that it had been he which should have redeemed Israel: and beside all this, to day is the third day since these things were done.

[22] Yea and certain women also of our company made us astonished, which were early at the sepulchre;

[23] And when they found not his body, they came, saying, that they had also seen a vision of angels, which said that he was alive.

[24] And certain of them which were with us went to the sepulchre and found it even so as the women had said: but him they saw not.

[25] Then he said unto them, O fools and slow of heart to believe all that the prophets have spoken:

[26] Ought not Christ to have suffered these things and to enter into his glory?

[27] And beginning at Moses and all the prophets, he expounded unto them in all the scriptures the things concerning himself.

Just as was pointed out in the previous chapter, the scripture helps provide the food needed for the Holy Spirit to feed our spirit. There will always be those trying to oppose God because of the spirit that drives them. He has allowed man's influence in the scripture by allowing man's own weakness to be used in His writings. Hence, the ability to understand scripture is inspired by God. Therefore, what we see in scripture is God blurred by man's knowledge, understanding and willingness at the time.

Just as what I am writing now is limited because I do not have a complete knowledge of God nor do I have a complete expertise in the use of the English language. So, I am putting the words God is inspiring me to use based on my understanding and my ability to receive of His intents in this book.

1 Corinthians 13:9-13 King James Version (KJV)
[9] For we know in part and we prophesy in part.
[10] But when that which is perfect is come, then that which is in part shall be done away.
[11] When I was a child, I spake as a child, I understood as a child, I thought as a child: but when I became a man, I put away childish things.
[12] For now we see through a glass, darkly; but then face to face: now I know in part; but then shall I know even as also I am known.
[13] And now abideth faith, hope, charity, these three; but the greatest of these is charity.

The Lord also wants me to point out that Satan tries to counterfeit the word of God and His ways. Be careful of those things you choose to allow to enter your mind because Satan wants to counterfeit God in your life so that you will miss the mark.

The scripture contains both the personality traits of man, the evil one and of God. It also includes the devil's dealings with man. Man's personality is shown as both good and bad. This is why just reading the words without the enlightenment of the Holy Spirit can lead to either good or evil. Thereby man falls short of God's original intent for its use for our good. The underlying truth is found in understanding the motivations and conditions of the people in the particular situation. Then one must evaluate God's intent and purposes by what is being said directed by the power of the Holy Spirit. Someone who is just reading the words can end up in choosing good or evil. This occurs when the choice is based solely on using his intelligence in understanding the situation without the guidance of the Holy Spirit. Remember that although the entirety of scripture has been provided for us to learn not everything included in scripture is there for us to emulate. Many situations were placed there so that we can learn what the results of choosing evil can produce. Many can quote the words of scripture, the chapter and verse, but they do not understand the true intent for which it is written. So, scripture without the insight of the Holy Spirit is without understanding. I have known many who can quote chapter and verse yet they lack understanding because they have chosen to use their own understanding and intelligence, not the work of the Holy Spirit.

Case in point, I was discussing the meaning of scripture and man's misuse of it with a young man. In this conversation, we started to discuss creation. He insisted that all scientist believe in God because scripture states God is the source of creation. I tried to explain to him that was not the case but he insisted that it was true. We all need to understand somewhere he has been misguided in his understanding of the work of and performance of scripture in the world around us. That is why you hear many different interpretations that abuse what God has provided. Consider the book Ester. God is not mentioned in the entire book, but His influence is all throughout the book and His presence is unmistakable if you choose to allow the Holy Spirit to aid you in finding it.

Proverbs 15:1-3 King James Version (KJV)
[1] A soft answer turneth away wrath: but grievous words stir up anger.
[2] The tongue of the wise useth knowledge aright: but the mouth of fools poureth out foolishness.
[3] The eyes of the Lord are in every place, beholding the evil and the good.

The saying "if something is used for something other than its intended purpose it is abuse" holds very true for scripture. It is an all too common occurrence. Even Satan tried to get Jesus to misuse scripture but Jesus knew scripture could not be used in an isolated instance. Jesus was able to draw on His knowledge of the entirety of scripture and God with the Holy Spirit. He then was able to interpret correctly the intent and purpose of not just an isolated single verse but also God's intent by providing a particular passage. Another case in point is that some interpret the scripture to say we must live in poverty while others interpret it to say we are to be rich. These are two extremes using the words of scripture but not the intent and purpose behind the scripture. It is not always readily discernable why some use the scripture for evil and others for good. The main point of the scripture is to get to know the ways of God and why man needs His help.

Scripture also acts as a check for our decisions by providing a standard of God's choices against the comparison of our choices. For example, many in this day and time many ask God if it is OK to have sex with someone they love outside of marriage (fornication). They usually reason that since they are "in love" it is OK, or they say in their own minds that God has provided permission. Scripture is very explicit on this matter and clearly states that sex outside of marriage is sin. Many enter in and stay in destructive relationships because they believe they are following scriptural mandates.

> **Acts 15:28-29 King James Version (KJV)**
> [28] For it seemed good to the Holy Ghost and to us, to lay upon you no greater burden than these necessary things;
> [29] That ye abstain from meats offered to idols and from blood and from things strangled and from fornication: from which if ye keep yourselves, ye shall do well. Fare ye well.

> **1 Corinthians 6:17-19 King James Version (KJV)**
> [17] But he that is joined unto the Lord is one spirit.
> [18] Flee fornication. Every sin that a man doeth is without the body; but he that committeth fornication sinneth against his own body.
> [19] What? know ye not that your body is the temple of the Holy Ghost which is in you, which ye have of God and ye are not your own?

God does not contradict Himself. He does not change. Remember there are three spirits in this world. The one we need to know and need to understand is God's voice, whether it is in scripture or him speaking to us.

> **Malachi 3:6 King James Version (KJV)**
> [6] For I am the Lord, I change not; therefore ye sons of Jacob are not consumed.

Satan will attempt to twist scripture and man can justify anything in his own mind. Many of us want to place blame for the results of our choices on everything but the fact that we made the choice. Just as Adam said it was the woman who made him do it. Adam's action caused his sin to be initiated. It was his choice to make and none could be blamed outside of himself no matter what the woman had chosen to do.

Proverbs 14:12 King James Version (KJV)
¹² There is a way which seemeth right unto a man, but the end thereof are the ways of death.

Proverbs 21:2 King James Version (KJV)
² Every way of a man is right in his own eyes: but the Lord pondereth the hearts.

Judges 21:25 King James Version (KJV)
²⁵ In those days there was no king in Israel: every man did that which was right in his own eyes.

Genesis 3:9-12 King James Version (KJV)
⁹ And the Lord God called unto Adam and said unto him, Where art thou?
¹⁰ And he said, I heard thy voice in the garden and I was afraid, because I was naked; and I hid myself.
¹¹ And he said, Who told thee that thou wast naked? Hast thou eaten of the tree, whereof I commanded thee that thou shouldest not eat?
¹² And the man said, The woman whom thou gavest to be with me, she gave me of the tree and I did eat.

May God provide you with His understanding by His grace as you pursue your journey to get to know our Savior and as you walk through this life!

I would like to point out that I have not used any other source other than scripture and the Holy Spirit to prepare this book. Yes, you may find that others have come to the same conclusions listed herein. That only proves God continues to be active in working in the life of man and is a confirmation that God has been my guide. As scripture states in the mouths of two or three are His truth confirmed.

Scripture References

Section 90 Doctrine & Covenants
[Sec 90:4b] Ye were also in the beginning with the Father; that which is Spirit, even the Spirit of
truth; and truth is knowledge of things as they are and as they were and as they are to come; and
whatsoever is more or less than this, is the spirit of that wicked one, who was a liar from the
beginning.
[Sec 90:4c] The Spirit of truth is of God. I am the Spirit of truth.
[Sec 90:4d] And John bore record of me, saying, He received a fullness of truth; yea, even of all

truth and no man receiveth a fullness unless he keepeth his commandments.
[Sec 90:4e] He that keepeth his commandments, receiveth truth and light, until he is glorified in
truth and knoweth all things.
[Sec 90:5a] Man was also in the beginning with God. Intelligence, or the light of truth, was not
created or made, neither indeed can be.
[Sec 90:5b] All truth is independent in that sphere in which God has placed it, to act for itself, as
all intelligence also, otherwise there is no existence.

Jeremiah 14:2-12 King James Version (KJV)

2 Judah mourneth and the gates thereof languish; they are black unto the ground; and the cry of Jerusalem is gone up.

3 And their nobles have sent their little ones to the waters: they came to the pits and found no water; they returned with their vessels empty; they were ashamed and confounded and covered their heads.

4 Because the ground is chapt, for there was no rain in the earth, the plowmen were ashamed, they covered their heads.

5 Yea, the hind also calved in the field and forsook it, because there was no grass.

6 And the wild asses did stand in the high places, they snuffed up the wind like dragons; their eyes did fail, because there was no grass.

7 O Lord, though our iniquities testify against us, do thou it for thy name's sake: for our backslidings are many; we have sinned against thee.

8 O the hope of Israel, the saviour thereof in time of trouble, why shouldest thou be as a stranger in the land and as a wayfaring man that turneth aside to tarry for a night?

9 Why shouldest thou be as a man astonied, as a mighty man that cannot save? yet thou, O Lord, art in the midst of us and we are called by thy name; leave us not.

10 Thus saith the Lord unto this people, Thus have they loved to wander, they have not refrained their feet, therefore the Lord doth not accept them; he will now remember their iniquity and visit their sins.

11 Then said the Lord unto me, Pray not for this people for their good.

12 When they fast, I will not hear their cry; and when they offer burnt offering and an oblation, I will not accept them: but I will consume them by the sword and by the famine and by the pestilence.

Matthew 22:9-19 King James Version (KJV)

9 Go ye therefore into the highways and as many as ye shall find, bid to the marriage.

10 So those servants went out into the highways and gathered together all as many as they found, both bad and good: and the wedding was furnished with guests.

11 And when the king came in to see the guests, he saw there a man which had not on a wedding garment:

12 And he saith unto him, Friend, how camest thou in hither not having a wedding garment? And he was speechless.

[13] Then said the king to the servants, Bind him hand and foot and take him away and cast him into outer darkness, there shall be weeping and gnashing of teeth.

[14] For many are called, but few are chosen.

[15] Then went the Pharisees and took counsel how they might entangle him in his talk.

[16] And they sent out unto him their disciples with the Herodians, saying, Master, we know that thou art true and teachest the way of God in truth, neither carest thou for any man: for thou regardest not the person of men.

[17] Tell us therefore, What thinkest thou? Is it lawful to give tribute unto Caesar, or not?

[18] But Jesus perceived their wickedness and said, Why tempt ye me, ye hypocrites?

[19] Shew me the tribute money. And they brought unto him a penny.

Joel 2:27-32 King James Version (KJV)

[27] And ye shall know that I am in the midst of Israel and that I am the Lord your God and none else: and my people shall never be ashamed.

[28] And it shall come to pass afterward, that I will pour out my spirit upon all flesh; and your sons and your daughters shall prophesy, your old men shall dream dreams, your young men shall see visions:

[29] And also upon the servants and upon the handmaids in those days will I pour out my spirit.

[30] And I will shew wonders in the heavens and in the earth, blood and fire and pillars of smoke.

[31] The sun shall be turned into darkness and the moon into blood, before the great and terrible day of the Lord come.

[32] And it shall come to pass, that whosoever shall call on the name of the Lord shall be delivered: for in mount Zion and in Jerusalem shall be deliverance, as the Lord hath said and in the remnant whom the Lord shall call.

Joel 3:1-5 King James Version (KJV)

[1] For, behold, in those days and in that time, when I shall bring again the captivity of Judah and Jerusalem,

[2] I will also gather all nations and will bring them down into the valley of Jehoshaphat and will plead with them there for my people and for my heritage Israel, whom they have scattered among the nations and parted my land.

[3] And they have cast lots for my people; and have given a boy for an harlot and sold a girl for wine, that they might drink.

[4] Yea and what have ye to do with me, O Tyre and Zidon and all the coasts of Palestine? will ye render me a recompence? and if ye recompense me, swiftly and speedily will I return your recompence upon your own head;

[5] Because ye have taken my silver and my gold and have carried into your temples my goodly pleasant things:

John 1:2-12 King James Version (KJV)

[2] The same was in the beginning with God.

[3] All things were made by him; and without him was not any thing made that was made.

[4] In him was life; and the life was the light of men.

[5] And the light shineth in darkness; and the darkness comprehended it not.

[6] There was a man sent from God, whose name was John.

[7] The same came for a witness, to bear witness of the Light, that all men through him might believe.

[8] He was not that Light, but was sent to bear witness of that Light.

[9] That was the true Light, which lighteth every man that cometh into the world.

[10] He was in the world and the world was made by him and the world knew him not.

[11] He came unto his own and his own received him not.

[12] But as many as received him, to them gave he power to become the sons of God, even to them that believe on his name:

John 3:16-20 King James Version (KJV)

[16] For God so loved the world, that he gave his only begotten Son, that whosoever believeth in him should not perish, but have everlasting life.

[17] For God sent not his Son into the world to condemn the world; but that the world through him might be saved.

[18] He that believeth on him is not condemned: but he that believeth not is condemned already, because he hath not believed in the name of the only begotten Son of God.

[19] And this is the condemnation, that light is come into the world and men loved darkness rather than light, because their deeds were evil.

[20] For every one that doeth evil hateth the light, neither cometh to the light, lest his deeds should be reproved.

John 5:31-41 King James Version (KJV)

[31] If I bear witness of myself, my witness is not true.

[32] There is another that beareth witness of me; and I know that the witness which he witnesseth of me is true.

[33] Ye sent unto John and he bare witness unto the truth.

[34] But I receive not testimony from man: but these things I say, that ye might be saved.

[35] He was a burning and a shining light: and ye were willing for a season to rejoice in his light.

[36] But I have greater witness than that of John: for the works which the Father hath given me to finish, the same works that I do, bear witness of me, that the Father hath sent me.

[37] And the Father himself, which hath sent me, hath borne witness of me. Ye have neither heard his voice at any time, nor seen his shape.

[38] And ye have not his word abiding in you: for whom he hath sent, him ye believe not.

[39] Search the scriptures; for in them ye think ye have eternal life: and they are they which testify of me.

[40] And ye will not come to me, that ye might have life.

[41] I receive not honour from men.

Acts 10:38-48 King James Version (KJV)

[38] How God anointed Jesus of Nazareth with the Holy Ghost and with power: who went about doing good and healing all that were oppressed of the devil; for God was with him.

[39] And we are witnesses of all things which he did both in the land of the Jews and in Jerusalem; whom they slew and hanged on a tree:

[40] Him God raised up the third day and shewed him openly;

[41] Not to all the people, but unto witnesses chosen before God, even to us, who did eat and drink with him after he rose from the dead.

[42] And he commanded us to preach unto the people and to testify that it is he which was ordained of God to be the Judge of quick and dead.

[43] To him give all the prophets witness, that through his name whosoever believeth in him shall receive remission of sins.

[44] While Peter yet spake these words, the Holy Ghost fell on all them which heard the word.

[45] And they of the circumcision which believed were astonished, as many as came with Peter, because that on the Gentiles also was poured out the gift of the Holy Ghost.

[46] For they heard them speak with tongues and magnify God. Then answered Peter,

[47] Can any man forbid water, that these should not be baptized, which have received the Holy Ghost as well as we?

[48] And he commanded them to be baptized in the name of the Lord. Then prayed they him to tarry certain days.

Romans 9:30-33 King James Version (KJV)

[30] What shall we say then? That the Gentiles, which followed not after righteousness, have attained to righteousness, even the righteousness which is of faith.

[31] But Israel, which followed after the law of righteousness, hath not attained to the law of righteousness.

[32] Wherefore? Because they sought it not by faith, but as it were by the works of the law. For they stumbled at that stumblingstone;

[33] As it is written, Behold, I lay in Sion a stumblingstone and rock of offence: and whosoever believeth on him shall not be ashamed.

Romans 10:1-7 King James Version (KJV)

[1] Brethren, my heart's desire and prayer to God for Israel is, that they might be saved.

[2] For I bear them record that they have a zeal of God, but not according to knowledge.

[3] For they being ignorant of God's righteousness and going about to establish their own righteousness, have not submitted themselves unto the righteousness of God.

[4] For Christ is the end of the law for righteousness to every one that believeth.

[5] For Moses describeth the righteousness which is of the law, That the man which doeth those things shall live by them.

[6] But the righteousness which is of faith speaketh on this wise, Say not in thine heart, Who shall ascend into heaven? (that is, to bring Christ down from above:)

7 Or, Who shall descend into the deep? (that is, to bring up Christ again from the dead.)

1 John 5:2-12 King James Version (KJV)

2By this we know that we love the children of God, when we love God and keep his commandments.

3For this is the love of God, that we keep his commandments: and his commandments are not grievous.

4For whatsoever is born of God overcometh the world: and this is the victory that overcometh the world, even our faith.

5Who is he that overcometh the world, but he that believeth that Jesus is the Son of God?

6This is he that came by water and blood, even Jesus Christ; not by water only, but by water and blood. And it is the Spirit that beareth witness, because the Spirit is truth.

7For there are three that bear record in heaven, the Father, the Word and the Holy Ghost: and these three are one.

8And there are three that bear witness in earth, the Spirit and the water and the blood: and these three agree in one.

9If we receive the witness of men, the witness of God is greater: for this is the witness of God which he hath testified of his Son.

10He that believeth on the Son of God hath the witness in himself: he that believeth not God hath made him a liar; because he believeth not the record that God gave of his Son.

11And this is the record, that God hath given to us eternal life and this life is in his Son.

12He that hath the Son hath life; and he that hath not the Son of God hath not life.

Matthew 22:24-34 King James Version (KJV)

24 Saying, Master, Moses said, If a man die, having no children, his brother shall marry his wife and raise up seed unto his brother.

25 Now there were with us seven brethren: and the first, when he had married a wife, deceased and, having no issue, left his wife unto his brother:

26 Likewise the second also and the third, unto the seventh.

27 And last of all the woman died also.

28 Therefore in the resurrection whose wife shall she be of the seven? for they all had her.

29 Jesus answered and said unto them, Ye do err, not knowing the scriptures, nor the power of God.

30 For in the resurrection they neither marry, nor are given in marriage, but are as the angels of God in heaven.

31 But as touching the resurrection of the dead, have ye not read that which was spoken unto you by God, saying,

32 I am the God of Abraham and the God of Isaac and the God of Jacob? God is not the God of the dead, but of the living.

33 And when the multitude heard this, they were astonished at his doctrine.

34 But when the Pharisees had heard that he had put the Sadducees to silence, they were gathered together.

Acts 18:19-28 King James Version (KJV)

[19] And he came to Ephesus and left them there: but he himself entered into the synagogue and reasoned with the Jews.

[20] When they desired him to tarry longer time with them, he consented not;

[21] But bade them farewell, saying, I must by all means keep this feast that cometh in Jerusalem: but I will return again unto you, if God will. And he sailed from Ephesus.

[22] And when he had landed at Caesarea and gone up and saluted the church, he went down to Antioch.

[23] And after he had spent some time there, he departed and went over all the country of Galatia and Phrygia in order, strengthening all the disciples.

[24] And a certain Jew named Apollos, born at Alexandria, an eloquent man and mighty in the scriptures, came to Ephesus.

[25] This man was instructed in the way of the Lord; and being fervent in the spirit, he spake and taught diligently the things of the Lord, knowing only the baptism of John.

[26] And he began to speak boldly in the synagogue: whom when Aquila and Priscilla had heard, they took him unto them and expounded unto him the way of God more perfectly.

[27] And when he was disposed to pass into Achaia, the brethren wrote, exhorting the disciples to receive him: who, when he was come, helped them much which had believed through grace:

[28] For he mightily convinced the Jews and that publicly, shewing by the scriptures that Jesus was Christ.

Romans 14:22-23 King James Version (KJV)

[22] Hast thou faith? have it to thyself before God. Happy is he that condemneth not himself in that thing which he alloweth.

[23] And he that doubteth is damned if he eat, because he eateth not of faith: for whatsoever is not of faith is sin.

Romans 15:1-9 King James Version (KJV)

[1] We then that are strong ought to bear the infirmities of the weak and not to please ourselves.

[2] Let every one of us please his neighbour for his good to edification.

[3] For even Christ pleased not himself; but, as it is written, The reproaches of them that reproached thee fell on me.

[4] For whatsoever things were written aforetime were written for our learning, that we through patience and comfort of the scriptures might have hope.

[5] Now the God of patience and consolation grant you to be likeminded one toward another according to Christ Jesus:

[6] That ye may with one mind and one mouth glorify God, even the Father of our Lord Jesus Christ.

[7] Wherefore receive ye one another, as Christ also received us to the glory of God.

[8] Now I say that Jesus Christ was a minister of the circumcision for the truth of God, to confirm the promises made unto the fathers:

[9] And that the Gentiles might glorify God for his mercy; as it is written, For this cause I will confess to thee among the Gentiles and sing unto thy name.

1 Timothy 4:8-16 King James Version (KJV)

[8]For bodily exercise profiteth little: but godliness is profitable unto all things, having promise of the life that now is and of that which is to come.
[9]This is a faithful saying and worthy of all acceptation
.[10]For therefore we both labour and suffer reproach, because we trust in the living God, who is the Saviour of all men, specially of those that believe.
[11]These things command and teach.
[12]Let no man despise thy youth; but be thou an example of the believers, in word, in conversation, in charity, in spirit, in faith, in purity.
[13]Till I come, give attendance to reading, to exhortation, to doctrine
[14]Neglect not the gift that is in thee, which was given thee by prophecy, with the laying on of the hands of the presbytery.
[15]Meditate upon these things; give thyself wholly to them; that thy profiting may appear to all
[16]Take heed unto thyself and unto the doctrine; continue in them: for in doing this thou shalt both save thyself and them that hear thee.

1 Timothy 5:1-2 King James Version (KJV)

[1]Rebuke not an elder, but intreat him as a father; and the younger men as brethren;
[2]The elder women as mothers; the younger as sisters, with all purity.

Matthew 4:4-25 King James Version (KJV)

[4]But he answered and said, It is written, Man shall not live by bread alone, but by every word that proceedeth out of the mouth of God.
[5]Then the devil taketh him up into the holy city and setteth him on a pinnacle of the temple,
[6]And saith unto him, If thou be the Son of God, cast thyself down: for it is written, He shall give his angels charge concerning thee: and in their hands they shall bear thee up, lest at any time thou dash thy foot against a stone.
[7]Jesus said unto him, It is written again, Thou shalt not tempt the Lord thy God.
[8]Again, the devil taketh him up into an exceeding high mountain and sheweth him all the kingdoms of the world and the glory of them;
[9]And saith unto him, All these things will I give thee, if thou wilt fall down and worship me.
[10]Then saith Jesus unto him, Get thee hence, Satan: for it is written, Thou shalt worship the Lord thy God and him only shalt thou serve.
[11]Then the devil leaveth him and, behold, angels came and ministered unto him.
[12]Now when Jesus had heard that John was cast into prison, he departed into Galilee;
[13]And leaving Nazareth, he came and dwelt in Capernaum, which is upon the sea coast, in the borders of Zabulon and Nephthalim:
[14]That it might be fulfilled which was spoken by Esaias the prophet, saying,
[15]The land of Zabulon and the land of Nephthalim, by the way of the sea, beyond Jordan, Galilee of the Gentiles;
[16]The people which sat in darkness saw great light; and to them which sat in the region and shadow of death light is sprung up.

[17] From that time Jesus began to preach and to say, Repent: for the kingdom of heaven is at hand.

[18] And Jesus, walking by the sea of Galilee, saw two brethren, Simon called Peter and Andrew his brother, casting a net into the sea: for they were fishers.

[19] And he saith unto them, Follow me and I will make you fishers of men.

[20] And they straightway left their nets and followed him.

[21] And going on from thence, he saw other two brethren, James the son of Zebedee and John his brother, in a ship with Zebedee their father, mending their nets; and he called them.

[22] And they immediately left the ship and their father and followed him.

[23] And Jesus went about all Galilee, teaching in their synagogues and preaching the gospel of the kingdom and healing all manner of sickness and all manner of disease among the people.

[24] And his fame went throughout all Syria: and they brought unto him all sick people that were taken with divers diseases and torments and those which were possessed with devils and those which were lunatick and those that had the palsy; and he healed them.

[25] And there followed him great multitudes of people from Galilee and from Decapolis and from Jerusalem and from Judaea and from beyond Jordan.

CHAPTER 4

Man Shall Not Tempt God

Deuteronomy 6:15-17 King James Version (KJV)
[15] (For the Lord thy God is a jealous God among you) lest the anger of the Lord thy God be kindled against thee and destroy thee from off the face of the earth.
[16] Ye shall not tempt the Lord your God, as ye tempted him in Massah.
[17] Ye shall diligently keep the commandments of the Lord your God and his testimonies and his statutes, which he hath commanded thee.

Exodus 17:6-7 King James Version (KJV)
[6] Behold, I will stand before thee there upon the rock in Horeb; and thou shalt smite the rock and there shall come water out of it, that the people may drink. And Moses did so in the sight of the elders of Israel.
[7] And he called the name of the place Massah and Meribah, because of the chiding of the children of Israel and because they tempted the Lord, saying, Is the Lord among us, or not?

The formula here is:

$$TIG = M \times C^2$$

Where:

TIG = Trust in God

M = man

C^2 = Christ X Comforter (the Holy Spirit)

The definition of tempting God is to deny that God is truly God or to show distrust in him. God does not tolerate distrust or tolerate unfaithfulness. This is the true meaning of Him being termed as being jealous. It is not jealous by our current definition but something that has do with our trust in him. I mean, who is there that God has to compete with him except in the mind of man. Trust in God can only be achieved or empowered through the regenerative work of Christ Jesus and the Holy Spirit. Without this duo working in tandem we cannot know the True God nor can we fully trust that he is or that He is, or that He will provide for our good.

Man has an issue. He wants his own way. This is so that he can be justified in what he does. This can be either to impress others or to have power over others. When we approach God, we can do so in complete submission or we can do so in a way in which we attempt to twist His arm. In doing this we try to trick him into performing acts that glorify man and not God. This was exemplified when Jesus was approached by Satan in the wilderness. He tried to have Jesus to influence God to perform an act that would glorify Jesus in the sight of man but not really profit God's kingdom or bring glory to God. Man is to make nothing including himself, as a God above the Lord our God. So if we misuse scripture for our own glory rather than the glory of God, we attempt to influence God to do something that is not the way the scripture was intended. Then this is considered tempting God or denying Him. Therefore, to go against the true purpose for which scripture has been provided is sin. In other words, we abuse the words of God by using them for a purpose for which they were not intended.

Matthew 4:11 King James Version (KJV)
4 But he answered and said, It is written, Man shall not live by bread alone, but by every word that proceedeth out of the mouth of God.
5 Then the devil taketh him up into the holy city and setteth him on a pinnacle of the temple,
6 And saith unto him, If thou be the Son of God, cast thyself down: for it is written, He shall give his angels charge concerning thee: and in their hands they shall bear thee up, lest at any time thou dash thy foot against a stone.
7 Jesus said unto him, It is written again, Thou shalt not tempt the Lord thy God.
8 Again, the devil taketh him up into an exceeding high mountain and sheweth him all the kingdoms of the world and the glory of them;
9 And saith unto him, All these things will I give thee, if thou wilt fall down and worship me.
10 Then saith Jesus unto him, Get thee hence, Satan: for it is written, Thou shalt worship the Lord thy God and him only shalt thou serve.
11 Then the devil leaveth him and, behold, angels came and ministered unto him.

Paul taught that he was free to do anything, but that not all things were beneficial for him. He is saying that we have the ability to choose whatever we want, good or evil, but the thing that we should choose is good.

1 Corinthians 6:11-13 Amplified Bible (AMP)
[11] And such were some of you [before you believed]. But you were washed [by the atoning sacrifice of Christ], you were sanctified [set apart for God and made holy], you were justified [declared free of guilt] in the name of the Lord Jesus Christ and in the [Holy] Spirit of our God [the source of the believer's new life and changed behavior]. The Body Is the Lord's
[12] Everything is permissible for me, but not all things are beneficial. Everything is permissible for me, but I will not be enslaved by anything [and brought under its power, allowing it to control me].
[13] Food is for the stomach and the stomach for food, but God will do away with both of them. The body is not intended for sexual immorality, but for the Lord and the Lord is for the body [to save, sanctify and raise it again because of the sacrifice of the cross].

Some of us seek the "fleece" experience, but is that any different from trying to use God's word for our own glory rather than God's glory? consider the prophet in Judges, who used a fleece to verify that God would honor His word because he did not trust that God would do as He had stated. Here God showed His willingness to put up with us and how compassionate He is. I guess I can say I was the same way when God told me to write this book. I doubted that it was really him telling me this but he provided verification through the inspiration of a fellow saint. It was truly an uplifting spiritual experience when I received this confirmation as my heart leaped for joy.

Judges 6:36-38 King James Version (KJV)
[36] And Gideon said unto God, If thou wilt save Israel by mine hand, as thou hast said,
[37] Behold, I will put a fleece of wool in the floor; and if the dew be on the fleece only and it be dry upon all the earth beside, then shall I know that thou wilt save Israel by mine hand, as thou hast said.
[38] And it was so: for he rose up early on the morrow and thrust the fleece together and wringed the dew out of the fleece, a bowl full of water.

As you can see by my testimonies, I am not yet perfect but I continue to strive for the high calling of Christ Jesus. I have been empowered through the works of the Holy Spirit to prove that God is real. God is patient with me and loves me enough to allow me to make mistakes.

Philippians 3:13-15 King James Version (KJV)

[13] Brethren, I count not myself to have apprehended: but this one thing I do, forgetting those things which are behind and reaching forth unto those things which are before,

[14] I press toward the mark for the prize of the high calling of God in Christ Jesus.

[15] Let us therefore, as many as be perfect, be thus minded: and if in any thing ye be otherwise minded, God shall reveal even this unto you.

CHAPTER 5

Thou Shalt Worship The Lord Thy God

The formula here is

TW = M X C²

Where

TW = True worship

M = Man

C² = Christ X the Comforter (the Holy Spirit)

There is a question we all have to answer. Why in the Ten Commandments do the first few all have to do with God? Let us review these commandments.

Exodus 20:1-17 King James Version (KJV)
[1] And God spake all these words, saying,
[2] I am the LORD thy God, which have brought thee out of the land of Egypt, out of the house of bondage.
[3] Thou shalt have no other gods before me.
[4] Thou shalt not make unto thee any graven image, or any likeness of any thing that is in heaven above, or that is in the earth beneath, or that is in the water under the earth.
[5] Thou shalt not bow down thyself to them, nor serve them: for I the LORD thy God am a jealous God, visiting the iniquity of the fathers upon the children unto the third and fourth generation of them that hate me;
[6] And shewing mercy unto thousands of them that love me and keep my commandments.

[7] Thou shalt not take the name of the Lᴏʀᴅ thy God in vain; for the Lᴏʀᴅ will not hold him guiltless that taketh his name in vain.

[8] Remember the sabbath day, to keep it holy.

[9] Six days shalt thou labour and do all thy work:

[10] But the seventh day is the sabbath of the Lᴏʀᴅ thy God: in it thou shalt not do any work, thou, nor thy son, nor thy daughter, thy manservant, nor thy maidservant, nor thy cattle, nor thy stranger that is within thy gates:

[11] For in six days the Lᴏʀᴅ made heaven and earth, the sea and all that in them is and rested the seventh day: wherefore the Lᴏʀᴅ blessed the sabbath day and hallowed it.

[12] Honour thy father and thy mother: that thy days may be long upon the land which the Lᴏʀᴅ thy God giveth thee.

[13] Thou shalt not kill.

[14] Thou shalt not commit adultery.

[15] Thou shalt not steal.

[16] Thou shalt not bear false witness against thy neighbour.

[17] Thou shalt not covet thy neighbour's house, thou shalt not covet thy neighbour's wife, nor his manservant, nor his maidservant, nor his ox, nor his ass, nor any thing that is thy neighbour's.

I guess I should point out these are the first Ten Commandments, not the only commandments in scripture, handed down by God. There was about 400 years between God's choice of Abraham as the father of His chosen people before these commandments were provided in written form. I can see, from the dealings of God with others prior to Abraham, there were those who had knowledge of these commandments before they were handed down by God through Moses. Consider both Melchizedek and Enoch. They both performed acts that were only provided in written form much later. They are not the only ones.

Genesis 14:17-19 King James Version (KJV)

[17] And the king of Sodom went out to meet him after his return from the slaughter of Chedorlaomer and of the kings that were with him, at the valley of Shaveh, which is the king's dale.

[18] And Melchizedek king of Salem brought forth bread and wine: and he was the priest of the most high God.

[19] And he blessed him and said, Blessed be Abram of the most high God, possessor of heaven and earth:

Genesis 5:23-25 King James Version (KJV)

[23] And all the days of Enoch were three hundred sixty and five years:

[24] And Enoch walked with God: and he was not; for God took him.

[25] And Methuselah lived an hundred eighty and seven years and begat Lamech.

These commandments were provided to God's people that they might be an example to the world of how God works with His people. This was to make them different or peculiar from the rest of the world. Therefore, they would be an example for the world to see how God works in the lives of those who love Him.

Deuteronomy 14:1-2 King James Version (KJV)

[1] Ye are the children of the Lord your God: ye shall not cut yourselves, nor make any baldness between your eyes for the dead.

[2] For thou art an holy people unto the Lord thy God and the Lord hath chosen thee to be a peculiar people unto himself, above all the nations that are upon the earth.

1 Peter 2:8-10 King James Version (KJV)

[8] And a stone of stumbling and a rock of offence, even to them which stumble at the word, being disobedient: whereunto also they were appointed.

[9] But ye are a chosen generation, a royal priesthood, an holy nation, a peculiar people; that ye should shew forth the praises of him who hath called you out of darkness into his marvellous light;

[10] Which in time past were not a people, but are now the people of God: which had not obtained mercy, but now have obtained mercy.

In the first four of the Ten Commandments, we see what is needed to keep our focus on God. The first one states that we are to have no other gods before him. A restatement is that God is the only God. Just as is stated in the Hebrew proclamation, which is titled the Shema (Hebrew for hear or listen and to pay particular attention). This commandment of God being the only god is actually reiterated in the first line of the Shema, "Hear O Israel, the Lord is our God, the Lord is One." The Shema is a biblical prayer that God's people were to pray morning and evening. It is still recited today in Jewish services. The word Shema is the Hebrew proclamation for "hear." It was God's way of telling His people to pay attention to the commandment and not just to quote a set of memorized words. When this is used, God is saying pay attention. It is more than quoting a set of memorized words. It is for us to learn that we are to focus on the fact that God is included in all of life.

Deuteronomy 5:32-33 King James Version (KJV)

[32] Ye shall observe to do therefore as the Lord your God hath commanded you: ye shall not turn aside to the right hand or to the left.

[33] Ye shall walk in all the ways which the Lord your God hath commanded you, that ye may live and that it may be well with you and that ye may prolong your days in the land which ye shall possess.

Deuteronomy 6:1-9 King James Version (KJV)

[1] Now these are the commandments, the statutes and the judgments, which the LORD your God commanded to teach you, that ye might do them in the land whither ye go to possess it:
[2] That thou mightest fear the LORD thy God, to keep all his statutes and his commandments, which I command thee, thou and thy son and thy son's son, all the days of thy life; and that thy days may be prolonged.
[3] Hear therefore, O Israel and observe to do it; that it may be well with thee and that ye may increase mightily, as the LORD God of thy fathers hath promised thee, in the land that floweth with milk and honey.

Verses 4 and 5 are the Shema that God's people were to quote each day.

[4] Hear, O Israel: The LORD our God is one LORD:
[5] And thou shalt love the LORD thy God with all thine heart and with all thy soul and with all thy might.
[6] And these words, which I command thee this day, shall be in thine heart:
[7] And thou shalt teach them diligently unto thy children and shalt talk of them when thou sittest in thine house and when thou walkest by the way and when thou liest down and when thou risest up.
[8] And thou shalt bind them for a sign upon thine hand and they shall be as frontlets between thine eyes.
[9] And thou shalt write them upon the posts of thy house and on thy gates.

Galatians 3:15-19 King James Version (KJV)

[15] Brethren, I speak after the manner of men; Though it be but a man's covenant, yet if it be confirmed, no man disannulleth, or addeth thereto.
[16] Now to Abraham and his seed were the promises made. He saith not, And to seeds, as of many; but as of one, And to thy seed, which is Christ.
[17] And this I say, that the covenant, that was confirmed before of God in Christ, the law, which was four hundred and thirty years after, cannot disannul, that it should make the promise of none effect.
[18] For if the inheritance be of the law, it is no more of promise: but God gave it to Abraham by promise.
[19] Wherefore then serveth the law? It was added because of transgressions, till the seed should come to whom the promise was made; and it was ordained by angels in the hand of a mediator.

There is some important instruction here that we need to pay attention to. Keep these things in your heart and recite them to your children when you are at home and away and to yourself when you lie down and rise. This is another way of saying our focus is never to be turned from God. This is true worship. We are to keep our attention on God wherever we are and in every phase of our lives. We are to teach this discipline to our children. This does not in any way prevent our children from exercising their free will but only enables them to make a more informed decision about following God.

I am led to share the following. The teaching of God's ways to my children was something that I, in my walk with God, did not pay a lot of attention to. Like a lot of us, I followed many of the popular trends of the day early on in their lives. One of which was to allow our children to make up their own minds and not to force our beliefs on them. What a devious tool that the evil one has used. You know how we in this country value our so-called freedom. This philosophy fit right into that niche. Once the Spirit was able to get me to see the error of my ways, he corrected my understanding. I am able to see now that following this twisted philosophy has had a profound effect on their walk with God. Like with all sin we are not always able to reverse the impact of our choices. Please do not make this mistake in your walk with God. If we do not instill the precepts of God in our kids, the forces of the spirits of the world will definitely instill theirs. The world refers to other people and Satan.

So now, let us get back to worship. First, our worship should be limited to God and him only. Jesus the Christ emphasized this. But, before I continue on this track, I need to point out in scripture the word for God is Elohim, which is a plural noun. Does this contradict the statement that God is one God? Well no, it does not for me. Jesus tells us that He, God and the Holy Spirit are one. My understanding of this is that they are inseparable and in complete agreement with each other. Yet they are individuals. There is a lot of conversation on this concept but the understanding the Lord has passed on to me is that the Godhead is individuals just as we are. This is explained to me by Jesus the Christ's statement that we should be one just as He and God and the Holy Spirit are one. In my understanding, they are in complete agreement and ideology yet still individuals. So, they have the same ideals, likes, dislikes, principles, goals and desires and they work to complement each other. There is no variation in them.

Luke 6:39-40 King James Version (KJV)
[39] And he spake a parable unto them, Can the blind lead the blind? shall they not both fall into the ditch?
[40] The disciple is not above his master: but every one that is perfect shall be as his master.

John 17:10-11 King James Version (KJV)
[10] And all mine are thine and thine are mine; and I am glorified in them.
[11] And now I am no more in the world, but these are in the world and I come to thee. Holy Father, keep through thine own name those whom thou hast given me, that they may be one, as we are.

This is a concept for me and you to understand. So, I will use and an example. Martin Luther King, in history is well known. The impact of what he did has been long lasting. His influence was infused with the power of the Spirit to get the populous to stand up for freedom and equality using peaceful non-violent protest. In today's world we see unity being attempted in the corporate and political climate without following of God's principles. It is about the corporate good not necessarily for the glory of God. As we can see, Martin Luther King through adherence to God's principles he was able to bring about a change that to that point in time was not allowed. I am also led to share the experience of the building of the tower of Babel. Here was a group that was focused on one goal. That goal was to prove that they could reach God by their own effort and not by the means He has provided. They were united in purpose but for the wrong reason.

The focus of worship is the Godhead, which is God, the Holy Spirit and Jesus the Christ.

So, let us see how the scripture describes worship. I will start at the end of the scripture, in Revelations, where we are told about creatures that are flying around the throne of God worshiping by saying "holy, holy, holy."

Revelation 4:4-11 King James Version (KJV)
[4] After this I looked and, behold, a door was opened in heaven: and the first voice which I heard was as it were of a trumpet talking with me; which said, Come up hither and I will shew thee things which must be hereafter.
[2] And immediately I was in the spirit: and, behold, a throne was set in heaven and one sat on the throne.

[3] And he that sat was to look upon like a jasper and a sardine stone: and there was a rainbow round about the throne, in sight like unto an emerald.

[4] And round about the throne were four and twenty seats: and upon the seats I saw four and twenty elders sitting, clothed in white raiment; and they had on their heads crowns of gold.

[5] And out of the throne proceeded lightnings and thunderings and voices: and there were seven lamps of fire burning before the throne, which are the seven Spirits of God.

[6] And before the throne there was a sea of glass like unto crystal: and in the midst of the throne and round about the throne, were four beasts full of eyes before and behind.

[7] And the first beast was like a lion and the second beast like a calf and the third beast had a face as a man and the fourth beast was like a flying eagle.

[8] And the four beasts had each of them six wings about him; and they were full of eyes within: and they rest not day and night, saying, Holy, holy, holy, LORD God Almighty, which was and is and is to come.

[9] And when those beasts give glory and honour and thanks to him that sat on the throne, who liveth for ever and ever,

[10] The four and twenty elders fall down before him that sat on the throne and worship him that liveth for ever and ever and cast their crowns before the throne, saying,

[11] Thou art worthy, O Lord, to receive glory and honour and power: for thou hast created all things and for thy pleasure they are and were created.

Here we see true worship. This is the recognition of God's attributes of Holiness and reverence to him. The dictionary defines holy as being perfect in goodness and righteousness but scripture says to be holy is to be set apart for God according to His righteousness. To be set apart for God means that, in the world, we are separate from the world but unified with God. Righteousness is to be in complete agreement with divine law. Here, in the following scripture, we see the recognition of God's immortal existence. We see that as creator of all things, He is worthy to receive honor, glory and praise because it is by His power all things exist and have their being. Think about the fact that God has placed in us the gift of life which began by His breath being placed in us and. Without our breathing in air and exhaling, we cannot survive. Every breath we take should help us to know that somewhere, somehow someone had the intelligence to cause us to exist. Our bodies were designed with many protective systems such as the way our heartbeat and breathing are involuntary. Which means they operate without our control. Yet most of us do not recognize that God is the power behind our existence and us.

Genesis 2:6-8 King James Version (KJV)
[6] But there went up a mist from the earth and watered the whole face of the ground.
[7] And the Lord God formed man of the dust of the ground and breathed into his nostrils the breath of life; and man became a living soul.
[8] And the Lord God planted a garden eastward in Eden; and there he put the man whom he had formed.

In the book of Revelations, we also see God is a living entity not an image or some lofty thought that we have or that we can create. Moreover, because of who He is, we do not have anything we can use, something made with our own hands, that can represent Him. We tend to focus our attention on the physical. This tendency will most likely cause us to misrepresent worship. Therefore, images are out of the question to represent God.

God has demonstrated in scripture that symbols (such as the cross and the serpent on the rod) can be used as reminders, but images are out of the question when it comes to truly representing God. Scripture states that God told Moses to have people to look on a rod with a serpent on it to be healed of snakebites because of their lack of faith in Him. We have to be careful with the use of pictures, statues and other objects we use to remind us God for we have a tendency to make them God and lose our focus of the true living God. We should recognize this tendency to worship the visible more than the invisible living God and guard against it. I know until the Lord provided me a more perfect image of Him I had this as a tendency in my life. I now refrain from the use of pictures and the like to be used in my worship. That is why I close my eyes when I pray, to blot out all around me except for God.

Numbers 21:8 King James Version (KJV)
[8] And the Lord said unto Moses, Make thee a fiery serpent and set it upon a pole: and it shall come to pass, that every one that is bitten, when he looketh upon it, shall live.

SUMMARY

Until we are in heaven with God worship on earth requires some preparation on our part. Worship is about more than what we do one hour per week. It is about what we do each day.

1. We are to be constantly drawn out in prayer and seeking the guidance of the Holy Spirit.

2. We are to study to learn more about God and the inner workings of His creation.

3. We are to seek how we are to serve Him.

4. We are to be constantly seeking to bring about His kingdom on this earth.

5. We are to allow His Holy Spirit to purge us constantly of all unrighteousness and all conduct which is indicative of iniquity in our lives.

6. We are to be clean in body, mind and Spirit so that God's presence can reside with us. The people of Israel were to clean their clothes, their bodies and seek forgiveness for sin before they could worship Him in His temple and before he would allow His presence to be there with them.

Exodus 19:9-11King James Version (KJV)
[9] And the Lord said unto Moses, Lo, I come unto thee in a thick cloud, that the people may hear when I speak with thee and believe thee for ever. And Moses told the words of the people unto the Lord.
[10] And the Lord said unto Moses, Go unto the people and sanctify them to day and to morrow and let them wash their clothes,
[11] And be ready against the third day: for the third day the Lord will come down in the sight of all the people upon mount Sinai.

Exodus 30:17-19 King James Version (KJV)
[17] And the Lord spake unto Moses, saying,
[18] Thou shalt also make a laver of brass and his foot also of brass, to wash withal: and thou shalt put it between the tabernacle of the congregation and the altar and thou shalt put water therein.
[19] For Aaron and his sons shall wash their hands and their feet thereat:

7. We are to do all that we can to set aside the day of worship to be with God and do nothing that will take away from that experience. As it states in scripture, set aside this day as Holy and do nothing except the Lord's work on this day.

Exodus 16:25-27 King James Version (KJV)
[25] And Moses said, Eat that to day; for to day is a sabbath unto the Lord: to day ye shall not find it in the field.

[26] Six days ye shall gather it; but on the seventh day, which is the sabbath, in it there shall be none.
[27] And it came to pass, that there went out some of the people on the seventh day for to gather and they found none.

Isaiah 58:12-14 King James Version (KJV)

[12] And they that shall be of thee shall build the old waste places: thou shalt raise up the foundations of many generations; and thou shalt be called, The repairer of the breach, The restorer of paths to dwell in.
[13] If thou turn away thy foot from the sabbath, from doing thy pleasure on my holy day; and call the sabbath a delight, the holy of the Lord, honourable; and shalt honour him, not doing thine own ways, nor finding thine own pleasure, nor speaking thine own words:
[14] Then shalt thou delight thyself in the Lord; and I will cause thee to ride upon the high places of the earth and feed thee with the heritage of Jacob thy father: for the mouth of the Lord hath spoken it.

When we come together, we should be ready to share in the unique gifts of the spirit that God has provided for each of us to edify the saints. We are to build up His body out of love for God and love for our brothers and sisters.

Be prepared to use the gifts of prophecy not only to call to repentance those who have not yet accepted Christ Jesus but also our fellow saints. This is so the Holy Spirit can reveal the secrets in their lives to them so that they will identify that God "is in our midst", repent and worship him.

The following are the principles of worship.

- Focus on God for who He is.
- Focus on God as Creator.
- Recognize that God is sovereign.
- Acknowledge that God's power sustains all things.
- Identify that for us to be allowed in His presence we are to be righteous and clean in body, mind and spirit.
- We are to be reverent toward him.
- We are to celebrate Him.
- Recognize our need for Him.
- We are to give thanks for His grace, compassion and gift of forgiveness in Christ Jesus.
- We come to learn more of Him.
- We come to serve Him by following His direction.

- We come to fellowship with Him and enjoy His presence.
- We come to confess our sin so that we can be cleansed through the forgiveness provided by Jesus Christ.
- We come to receive His healing of body, mind and spirit for the showing forth of His glory.
- We come to enjoy fellowship with Him and our fellow saints.
- We come to receive His direction and correction when needed.

None of this can happen without us repenting and receiving the forgiveness provided by Christ Jesus who empowers us through His Holy Spirit to be righteous and to serve God. When we allow contention, strife, envy, self-serving desires, dissension and other works of the flesh to inhabit our worship; or when we try to force our will on others the flow of the Holy Spirit will stop. He will not dwell in the midst of unrighteousness. Without the power of the Holy Spirit, we are just having a meeting not worshiping. These things can be eliminated when we seek the Holy Spirit to remove these things from our lives. Worship requires that we allow the Holy Spirit to put the right spirit in us. Then we can properly come together corporately and truly worship.

1 Corinthians 3:1-3 King James Version (KJV)
¹ And I, brethren, could not speak unto you as unto spiritual, but as unto carnal, even as unto babes in Christ.
² I have fed you with milk and not with meat: for hitherto ye were not able to bear it, neither yet now are ye able.
³ For ye are yet carnal: for whereas there is among you envying and strife and divisions, are ye not carnal and walk as men?

Some of us may not be aware that these unrighteous traits are part of us so we need to fast and pray for God to expose these in us. This opens the pathway for Him to cleanse us of all unrighteousness and to remove these characteristics from our lives. We cannot do this on our own, only through the power of the Holy Spirit can this be done.

CHAPTER 6

Repentance Required

The formula here is

TR = M X C²

Where

TR = True Repentance

M = Man

C² = Christ X the Comforter (the Holy Spirit)

Most have heard the phrase "my way or the highway." This phrase demonstrates the way many of us think. We want to do what we want, which is not always best for us. Consider the following scripture.

Matthew 7:9-19 King James Version (KJV)
⁹ Or what man is there of you, whom if his son ask bread, will he give him a stone?
¹⁰ Or if he ask a fish, will he give him a serpent?
¹¹ If ye then, being evil, know how to give good gifts unto your children, how much more shall your Father which is in heaven give good things to them that ask him?
¹² Therefore all things whatsoever ye would that men should do to you, do ye even so to them: for this is the law and the prophets.
¹³ Enter ye in at the strait gate: for wide is the gate and broad is the way, that leadeth to destruction and many there be which go in thereat:
¹⁴ Because strait is the gate and narrow is the way, which leadeth unto life and few there be that find it.
¹⁵ Beware of false prophets, which come to you in sheep's clothing, but inwardly they are ravening wolves.
¹⁶ Ye shall know them by their fruits. Do men gather grapes of thorns, or figs of thistles?

[17] Even so every good tree bringeth forth good fruit; but a corrupt tree bringeth forth evil fruit.

[18] A good tree cannot bring forth evil fruit, neither can a corrupt tree bring forth good fruit.

[19] Every tree that bringeth not forth good fruit is hewn down and cast into the fire.

Luke 13:19-29 King James Version (KJV)

[19] It is like a grain of mustard seed, which a man took and cast into his garden; and it grew and waxed a great tree; and the fowls of the air lodged in the branches of it.

[20] And again he said, Whereunto shall I liken the kingdom of God?

[21] It is like leaven, which a woman took and hid in three measures of meal, till the whole was leavened.

[22] And he went through the cities and villages, teaching and journeying toward Jerusalem.

[23] Then said one unto him, Lord, are there few that be saved? And he said unto them,

[24] Strive to enter in at the strait gate: for many, I say unto you, will seek to enter in and shall not be able.

[25] When once the master of the house is risen up and hath shut to the door and ye begin to stand without and to knock at the door, saying, Lord, Lord, open unto us; and he shall answer and say unto you, I know you not whence ye are:

[26] Then shall ye begin to say, We have eaten and drunk in thy presence and thou hast taught in our streets.

[27] But he shall say, I tell you, I know you not whence ye are; depart from me, all ye workers of iniquity.

[28] There shall be weeping and gnashing of teeth, when ye shall see Abraham and Isaac and Jacob and all the prophets, in the kingdom of God and you yourselves thrust out.

[29] And they shall come from the east and from the west and from the north and from the south and shall sit down in the kingdom of God.

Jesus the Christ talks about a gate. What does He mean by this? He is talking to the Jews but He is also including all other people not of the Jewish race. We see in scripture that God has provided a way to enter into His presence but not everyone will make that choice. Today, we hear many excuses from those who have heard about the forgiveness Christ Jesus offers, but have yet to accept it. The most common misconceptions are the behaviors of Christians do not portray the teachings of Jesus Christ, that the bible has so many errors and belief in God is based on superstitions. So how do we make this choice? We must look to God's ways rather than the way man behaves. We do this by making a conscious choice. First is the step of repentance. How is this described in scripture?

1 Kings 8:42-52 King James Version (KJV)

[42] (For they shall hear of thy great name and of thy strong hand and of thy stretched out arm;) when he shall come and pray toward this house;

[43] Hear thou in heaven thy dwelling place and do according to all that the stranger calleth to thee for: that all people of the earth may know thy name, to fear thee, as do thy people Israel; and that they may know that this house, which I have builded, is called by thy name.

[44] If thy people go out to battle against their enemy, whithersoever thou shalt send them and shall pray unto the Lord toward the city which thou hast chosen and toward the house that I have built for thy name:

[45] Then hear thou in heaven their prayer and their supplication and maintain their cause.

[46] If they sin against thee, (for there is no man that sinneth not,) and thou be angry with them and deliver them to the enemy, so that they carry them away captives unto the land of the enemy, far or near;

[47] Yet if they shall bethink themselves in the land whither they were carried captives and repent and make supplication unto thee in the land of them that carried them captives, saying, We have sinned and have done perversely, we have committed wickedness;

[48] And so return unto thee with all their heart and with all their soul, in the land of their enemies, which led them away captive and pray unto thee toward their land, which thou gavest unto their fathers, the city which thou hast chosen and the house which I have built for thy name:

[49] Then hear thou their prayer and their supplication in heaven thy dwelling place and maintain their cause,

[50] And forgive thy people that have sinned against thee and all their transgressions wherein they have transgressed against thee and give them compassion before them who carried them captive, that they may have compassion on them:

[51] For they be thy people and thine inheritance, which thou broughtest forth out of Egypt, from the midst of the furnace of iron:

[52] That thine eyes may be open unto the supplication of thy servant and unto the supplication of thy people Israel, to hearken unto them in all that they call for unto thee.

Here you can see God calling Israel to repent through the king to stop sinning. He calls them to first recognize and admit that they have done wrong and acted in wicked ways. Then God will hear them and will heal them. It should be pointed out that this is more than a verbal thing but a genuine willingness to desire to change their ways. See how Jesus puts it:

Matthew 9:12-13 King James Version (KJV)

[12] But when Jesus heard that, he said unto them, They that be whole need not a physician, but they that are sick.

[13] But go ye and learn what that meaneth, I will have mercy and not sacrifice: for I am not come to call the righteous, but sinners to repentance.

Matthew 3:7-9 King James Version (KJV)

[7] But when he saw many of the Pharisees and Sadducees come to his baptism, he said unto them, O generation of vipers, who hath warned you to flee from the wrath to come?

[8] Bring forth therefore fruits meet for repentance:

[9] And think not to say within yourselves, We have Abraham to our father: for I say unto you, that God is able of these stones to raise up children unto Abraham.

Matthew 21:28-30 King James Version (KJV)

[28] But what think ye? A certain man had two sons; and he came to the first and said, Son, go work to day in my vineyard.

[29] He answered and said, I will not: but afterward he repented and went.

[30] And he came to the second and said likewise. And he answered and said, I go, sir: and went not.

In each of these, we see that Jesus taught that repentance is about realizing we are doing wrong and then acting to reverse the behavior. So, we are not justified by status, race or religion. This is only done through our conscious choice to serve Him and by allowing His Holy Spirit to transform us. Consider the instruction Paul provides to the church. He advises the use of prophecy in love to identify secrets in individual's lives so that they will have to admit God is real and realize that they need to confess their sins before Him.

1 Corinthians 14:21-26 King James Version (KJV)

[21] In the law it is written, With men of other tongues and other lips will I speak unto this people; and yet for all that will they not hear me, saith the Lord.

[22] Wherefore tongues are for a sign, not to them that believe, but to them that believe not: but prophesying serveth not for them that believe not, but for them which believe.

[23] If therefore the whole church be come together into one place and all speak with tongues and there come in those that are unlearned, or unbelievers, will they not say that ye are mad?

[24] But if all prophesy and there come in one that believeth not, or one unlearned, he is convinced of all, he is judged of all:

[25] And thus are the secrets of his heart made manifest; and so falling down on his face he will worship God and report that God is in you of a truth.

[26] How is it then, brethren? when ye come together, every one of you hath a psalm, hath a doctrine, hath a tongue, hath a revelation, hath an interpretation. Let all things be done unto edifying.

Some time ago while on my way to the airport to drop my daughters off for an engagement, the Holy Spirit opened my insight to some scriptural instructions that I had been overlooking. This has to do with the method we should be using to bring converts into the church through allowing the Holy Spirit to bring them to repentance. We have had many programs for increasing church membership. All of these have had limited success. In scripture there is a model that the Lord has provided which will work for those who are willing to accept him. The model is a simple one. It is centered on the work of the Holy Spirit. We see this being used many places in scripture such as when the prophet Nathan told David about his sin with Bathsheba.

2 Samuel 12King James Version (KJV)

[12] And the Lord sent Nathan unto David. And he came unto him and said unto him, There were two men in one city; the one rich and the other poor.

[2] The rich man had exceeding many flocks and herds:

[3] But the poor man had nothing, save one little ewe lamb, which he had bought and nourished up: and it grew up together with him and with his children; it did eat of his own meat and drank of his own cup and lay in his bosom and was unto him as a daughter.

[4] And there came a traveller unto the rich man and he spared to take of his own flock and of his own herd, to dress for the wayfaring man that was come unto him; but took the poor man's lamb and dressed it for the man that was come to him.

[5] And David's anger was greatly kindled against the man; and he said to Nathan, As the Lord liveth, the man that hath done this thing shall surely die:

[6] And he shall restore the lamb fourfold, because he did this thing and because he had no pity.

[7] And Nathan said to David, Thou art the man. Thus saith the Lord God of Israel, I anointed thee king over Israel and I delivered thee out of the hand of Saul;

[8] And I gave thee thy master's house and thy master's wives into thy bosom and gave thee the house of Israel and of Judah; and if that had been too little, I would moreover have given unto thee such and such things.

[9] Wherefore hast thou despised the commandment of the Lord, to do evil in his sight? thou hast killed Uriah the Hittite with the sword and hast taken his wife to be thy wife and hast slain him with the sword of the children of Ammon.

[10] Now therefore the sword shall never depart from thine house; because thou hast despised me and hast taken the wife of Uriah the Hittite to be thy wife.

Jesus demonstrated this same gift of prophecy in His encounter with the woman at the well. He approached the Samaritan woman and had a conversation with her. In the conversation, he did something miraculous. He started exposing her secrets (the details about her life that a stranger could not have known). She was a woman who had been married several times but now she was living with a man who was not her husband. This was a sin. In doing this, Jesus showed us that prophecy is a method of evangelism that will work for those who are willing to receive it. These steps are further outlined in detail in the following scriptures:

John 4:6-28 King James Version (KJV)

[6] Now Jacob's well was there. Jesus therefore, being wearied with his journey, sat thus on the well: and it was about the sixth hour.

[7] There cometh a woman of Samaria to draw water: Jesus saith unto her, Give me to drink.

[8] (For his disciples were gone away unto the city to buy meat.)

[9] Then saith the woman of Samaria unto him, How is it that thou, being a Jew, askest drink of me, which am a woman of Samaria? for the Jews have no dealings with the Samaritans.

[10] Jesus answered and said unto her, If thou knewest the gift of God and who it is that saith to thee, Give me to drink; thou wouldest have asked of him and he would have given thee living water.

[11] The woman saith unto him, Sir, thou hast nothing to draw with and the well is deep: from whence then hast thou that living water?

[12] Art thou greater than our father Jacob, which gave us the well and drank thereof himself and his children and his cattle?

[13] Jesus answered and said unto her, Whosoever drinketh of this water shall thirst again:

[14] But whosoever drinketh of the water that I shall give him shall never thirst; but the water that I shall give him shall be in him a well of water springing up into everlasting life.

[15] The woman saith unto him, Sir, give me this water, that I thirst not, neither come hither to draw.

[16] Jesus saith unto her, Go, call thy husband and come hither.

[17] The woman answered and said, I have no husband. Jesus said unto her, Thou hast well said, I have no husband:

[18] For thou hast had five husbands; and he whom thou now hast is not thy husband: in that saidst thou truly.

[19] The woman saith unto him, Sir, I perceive that thou art a prophet.

[20] Our fathers worshipped in this mountain; and ye say, that in Jerusalem is the place where men ought to worship.

²¹ Jesus saith unto her, Woman, believe me, the hour cometh, when ye shall neither in this mountain, nor yet at Jerusalem, worship the Father.
²² Ye worship ye know not what: we know what we worship: for salvation is of the Jews.
²³ But the hour cometh and now is, when the true worshippers shall worship the Father in spirit and in truth: for the Father seeketh such to worship him.
²⁴ God is a Spirit: and they that worship him must worship him in spirit and in truth.
²⁵ The woman saith unto him, I know that Messias cometh, which is called Christ: when he is come, he will tell us all things.
²⁶ Jesus saith unto her, I that speak unto thee am he.
²⁷ And upon this came his disciples and marvelled that he talked with the woman: yet no man said, What seekest thou? or, Why talkest thou with her?
²⁸ The woman then left her waterpot and went her way into the city and saith to the men,

We in the church have been reluctant to allow the Holy Spirit to work one of the most enduring tasks that He can perform. We have set up an atmosphere where we limit His functionality. We have been reluctant to operate in the gifts of the spirit for fear that we cannot control them but how wrong we have been! We can see in the above scripture that the Holy Spirit controlled this whole discourse. As a result, the woman at the well was converted and became a missionary for the work of the Lord. We have become so sophisticated in our approach of the gospel that we feel we can do things in our own will and power. That puts the Lord on the sidelines (meaning we have left Him out of the process). This has set us up for failure.

Luke 8:16-18 King James Version (KJV)
¹⁶ No man, when he hath lighted a candle, covereth it with a vessel, or putteth it under a bed; but setteth it on a candlestick, that they which enter in may see the light.
¹⁷ For nothing is secret, that shall not be made manifest; neither any thing hid, that shall not be known and come abroad.
¹⁸ Take heed therefore how ye hear: for whosoever hath, to him shall be given; and whosoever hath not, from him shall be taken even that which he seemeth to have.

1 Corinthians 14:21-26 King James Version (KJV)
²¹ In the law it is written, With men of other tongues and other lips will I speak unto this people; and yet for all that will they not hear me, saith the Lord.
²² Wherefore tongues are for a sign, not to them that believe, but to them that believe not: but prophesying serveth not for them that believe not, but for them which believe.

23 If therefore the whole church be come together into one place and all speak with tongues and there come in those that are unlearned, or unbelievers, will they not say that ye are mad?
24 But if all prophesy and there come in one that believeth not, or one unlearned, he is convinced of all, he is judged of all:
25 And thus are the secrets of his heart made manifest; and so falling down on his face he will worship God and report that God is in you of a truth.
26 How is it then, brethren? when ye come together, every one of you hath a psalm, hath a doctrine, hath a tongue, hath a revelation, hath an interpretation. Let all things be done unto edifying.

It is a work of the Holy Spirit that is needed to bring converts to Christ. He must guide our part, as He will do the transforming work. Key points from the scripture above and the account of Jesus at the well are this:

1. We need to operate in the gift of prophecy though prayer and fasting.
2. The gift of prophecy will identify that God is among us and we are His followers.
3. When we operate in this gift, the Lord will provide us the things to say which will tactfully expose secrets of the individual. If they are willing to repent, the Holy Spirit can work in their life to bring them to God.

The work of the Holy Spirit on the day of Pentecost in the lives of those who were willing is now well studied but not often copied. Here we see how God using the power of the Holy Spirit can ignite men to respond to His call of repentance and how the Holy spirit transforms people. This demonstrates that spirit brings about spiritual transformation.

Oh, this is such a simple procedure. However, we in the church have not followed this because we do not want to make public peoples innermost secrets. We feel that is a no-no but that is not how God wants it. In fact, it is how He has to work. We have been so conditioned to the way the world operates that we have set the gospel instruction aside and have been working in our own strength and power. That has provided limited success. We need to reverse this trend and not be bound by political correctness or by trying to avoid embarrassment. God wants the secrets of men exposed because he wants us to be open with each other. Only when this occurs can the Holy Spirit work among us to function in spirit and in truth. Members should not be walking around on tiptoes or be afraid that they will not be accepted because of their past. As scripture states, all secrets will eventually be known. When all is exposed, no one will have anything to hide or fear. The Spirit awaits a people willing to be bold in the sharing of His work. We also must accept that not everyone is written in the Lamb's book of life. However, there are many He is waiting for us to visit so that they may be part of the kingdom here on earth. Additionally, this work is not limited to those outside the church. We in the church are called to allow this same experience in our lives.

James 5:11-20 King James Version (KJV)

[11] Behold, we count them happy which endure. Ye have heard of the patience of Job and have seen the end of the Lord; that the Lord is very pitiful and of tender mercy.

[12] But above all things, my brethren, swear not, neither by heaven, neither by the earth, neither by any other oath: but let your yea be yea; and your nay, nay; lest ye fall into condemnation.

[13] Is any among you afflicted? let him pray. Is any merry? let him sing psalms.
[14] Is any sick among you? let him call for the elders of the church; and let them pray over him, anointing him with oil in the name of the Lord:

[15] And the prayer of faith shall save the sick and the Lord shall raise him up; and if he have committed sins, they shall be forgiven him.

[16] Confess your faults one to another and pray one for another, that ye may be healed. The effectual fervent prayer of a righteous man availeth much.

[17] Elias was a man subject to like passions as we are and he prayed earnestly that it might not rain: and it rained not on the earth by the space of three years and six months.

[18] And he prayed again and the heaven gave rain and the earth brought forth her fruit.

[19] Brethren, if any of you do err from the truth and one convert him;
[20] Let him know, that he which converteth the sinner from the error of his way shall save a soul from death and shall hide a multitude of sins.

We are called to confess our sins openly to open us up to the work of the Holy Spirit so that he will transform and cleanse us from all sin and all unrighteousness. The open confession of sins has been discouraged in modern church. The closest example we have today is the use of the confessional in the Catholic Church. This has been modified from the instruction in scripture (It is now secret between the priest and the person doing the confession, not done openly to the entire church). Here the priest provides a solution for absolution for sins committed. It is not the Holy Spirit transforming the individual.

We have to recognize that many of the commands of scripture have been either ignored or modified to suit man's way of doing things and not done the way directed by God. The church needs to understand God has provided these instructions so that the intended purpose can be accomplished. Only by the work of the Holy Spirit can the true work of cleansing be accomplished. Until we are willing to follow God's direction fully this cannot be done.

I can remember when I tried to perform open confession in one of our prayer services. I was quickly admonished and told this was unacceptable. I was told the matter was between me and God not to be discussed openly. We need to recognize Satan is at work in the church trying to disrupt and halt the work of God.

When serving as pastor I saw many members who were hiding their sins or what they considered sin. I found members who secretly smoked because this was considered unacceptable behavior. Others were abusers of their wives and children. Some were fornicators and adulterers. We have given in to those things considered politically correct. We try to avoid exposing those things which we feel will open us up to litigation. Well the only thing we should fear is the wrath of God for preventing His Holy Spirit from functioning to make us a people acceptable to Him. It takes more than the sinner's prayer for the Holy Spirit to work in our lives.

Psalm 19:13-14 King James Version (KJV)
[13] Keep back thy servant also from presumptuous sins; let them not have dominion over me: then shall I be upright and I shall be innocent from the great transgression.
[14] Let the words of my mouth and the meditation of my heart, be acceptable in thy sight, O Lord, my strength and my redeemer.

Romans 12:1-3 King James Version (KJV)
[1] I beseech you therefore, brethren, by the mercies of God, that ye present your bodies a living sacrifice, holy, acceptable unto God, which is your reasonable service.

² And be not conformed to this world: but be ye transformed by the renewing of your mind, that ye may prove what is that good and acceptable and perfect, will of God.

³ For I say, through the grace given unto me, to every man that is among you, not to think of himself more highly than he ought to think; but to think soberly, according as God hath dealt to every man the measure of faith.

SUMMARY

God wants more than our minds to be changed He wants the renewal of our minds and spirit in the right way. That can only be performed by the power of the Holy Spirit. I do not want you to feel that we are going to lose our salvation but until we change the way we approach our commitment to Jesus Christ we will delay His coming and the building of His kingdom. We need to be aware of and follow the steps, the formula, he has provided for this to happen. It will not occur any other way.

I am prompted to share this testimony. As a new convert (when I first accepted baptism) because of my study of the scripture, prior to joining this church, I expected everyone in this church to be perfect and endowed with all the spiritual gifts. After being in the church for a year, I found this was definitely not the case. These people were *nothing* like what I was expecting! I decided to leave the church for that reason. Then at what I had determined would be my last service in this church something miraculous happened. While the closing prayer was being said, the lord spoke to me in an audible voice. He said, "If you were baptized unto a church." Then there was a period of silence. Then He said, "If you were baptized unto Me then you are in this for eternity." It was evident that the only viable choice for me was to honor my commitment to Christ Jesus and stay in this church because the first and only time I had been baptized was in this church. I realized, through the enlightenment of the Holy Spirit, that I was no different from any of those I was judging. They needed the work of Christ Jesus as much as I did. From then on, He has continued the transformation of my life from the selfish self-seeking Lorenzo to something entirely different. This is one reason giving a sermon is more than a speech. It is evidence that the life-giving blood of Christ Jesus empowered by the Holy Spirit really can convert us into a righteous people who can be empowered to build His kingdom on earth as it is in heaven. It is the evidence of the true call to repentance.

CHAPTER 7

Seek Ye First The Kingdom Of God

Matthew 6:28-34 King James Version (KJV)

[28] And why take ye thought for raiment? Consider the lilies of the field, how they grow; they toil not, neither do they spin:

[29] And yet I say unto you, That even Solomon in all his glory was not arrayed like one of these.

[30] Wherefore, if God so clothe the grass of the field, which to day is and to morrow is cast into the oven, shall he not much more clothe you, O ye of little faith?

[31] Therefore take no thought, saying, What shall we eat? or, What shall we drink? or, Wherewithal shall we be clothed?

[32] (For after all these things do the Gentiles seek:) for your heavenly Father knoweth that ye have need of all these things.

[33] But seek ye first the kingdom of God and his righteousness; and all these things shall be added unto you.

[34] Take therefore no thought for the morrow: for the morrow shall take thought for the things of itself. Sufficient unto the day is the evil thereof.

The formula here is

KG = M X C²

Where:

KG = Kingdom of God

M = Man

C² = Christ X the Comforter (the Holy Spirit)

For man to achieve **The Kingdom** requires that man be converted through the power of the Holy Spirit. It cannot be achieved any other way. Neither can the will power or the ingenuity of man accomplish this task. Man, without God, can only do things that are imperfect. This is because man is imperfect. Therefore, man's attempts at attaining **The Kingdom** all fall short.

The inspiration I have on this is as follows:

We need to make God a priority in our life. The issue is that we have set a goal to live our lives for our benefit and comfort rather than as God wants them to be. This translates into Me, My and Mine, my selfish motives. This has been an issue since the Garden of Eden.

We adapt our lives to adhere to the environment in which we are raised and/or based on our own personality. We usually choose those things that appeal to us to live our lives by, be it behaviors or actions or societal norms. These are what scripture terms as fleshly desires. Now we all have basic needs; food, shelter and clothing. However, in our country, we have established a level for these far and beyond what is considered basic. We live by Me, My and Mine. More is the norm in our society. The entire advertising industry is predicated on the premise that we are not complete without the products they are promoting. It is an appeal to our selfish nature.

I would like to call your attention to the hippy movement. A movement where people shunned the societal norms for possessions and what were considered the norms for morality. Its theme was love and freedom to do those things that made us feel good. Love everybody and everything, do not live as your parents just be free to be and do what makes you happy. Drugs, alcohol, sex and uninhibited life styles were promoted. On the opposite side, the religious end, we have also seen the monastic movement that shunned societal norms and sought to separate people from the world (everyday life of man). Yet even here, **The Kingdom** was normally missed. Neither of these met the call to **The Kingdom**. The problem was that this was not a voluntary turn to God but a man led attempt to get to **The Kingdom.** This is what man considers Utopia. Those involved did not really understand what was needed as a basis for this to occur, seeking without finding. Somehow, the Holy Spirit was not involved in the entire process, as was described by Jesus when he provided the parable of the sower.

John 3:6 King James Version (KJV)
[6] That which is born of the flesh is flesh; and that which is born of the Spirit is spirit.

One day at church while listening to our pastor's sermon, he used this scripture. It captivated me. All that week I could not get it off my mind. As usual, as He often does, it was the Holy Spirit teaching me more about God. I had a slight insight into the meaning of the scripture. Then all of a sudden, I was able to see it in terms of the way God wanted me to see it. This scripture states that we live our lives based on the spirit we are ruled by, or rather, we live our lives by the ruling authority in our lives. Scripture also states we are ruled by lusts of the flesh. Flesh is the spirit of man or the spirit of the evil one. Since we are human (flesh), we live in accordance with human desires and weaknesses and our goals are based on the desires and principles which we adhere to. As previously stated we are driven by the call of Me, My and Mine. Therefore, our number one goal is based on our personal wants and desires. These are usually all about self-aggrandizement or self-expansion of power, wealth, rank, or honor above that which is deserved or required. Just consider how each time Israel was called to rebuild the temple they got side tracked by the desire to look after their own personal comforts. So instead of following God's purpose for their return from captivity they made their own desires for comfort primary rather than God's purposes.

This is experienced in both secular and religious contexts because if the goal of what we do is about self-aggrandizement then result is the same. We cannot achieve the spiritual nature God desires us to achieve without the guidance of the Holy Spirit. That is the reason that God states that those who have done what we consider good deeds but have not love have never known Him. The good they do is for nothing and is as filthy rags. It is about a people driven by self-seeking principles rather than having in-depth love which glorifies God as the true motive. Therefore, when guided by those things which are all about self then the flesh rules.

When the Holy Spirit guides us, the Spirit rules by the power of God's love. God's love reigns and He is glorified.

3 John 11:11 King James Version (KJV)
[11] Beloved, follow not that which is evil, but that which is good. He that doeth good is of God: but he that doeth evil hath not seen God.

1 Corinthians 13:3 King James Version (KJV)
[3] And though I bestow all my goods to feed the poor and though I give my body to be burned and have not charity, it profiteth me nothing.

Mark 10:14King James Version (KJV)
[14] But when Jesus saw it, he was much displeased and said unto them, Suffer the little children to come unto me and forbid them not: for of such is the kingdom of God.

Luke 18:17King James Version (KJV)
[17] Verily I say unto you, Whosoever shall not receive the kingdom of God as a little child shall in no wise enter therein.

John 3:3King James Version (KJV)
[3] Jesus answered and said unto him, Verily, verily, I say unto thee, Except a man be born again, he cannot see the kingdom of God.

Romans 14:17 King James Version (KJV)
[17] For the kingdom of God is not meat and drink; but righteousness and peace and joy in the Holy Ghost.

Galatians 5:19-21 King James Version (KJV)
[19] Now the works of the flesh are manifest, which are these; Adultery, fornication, uncleanness, lasciviousness,
[20] Idolatry, witchcraft, hatred, variance, emulations, wrath, strife, seditions, heresies,
[21] Envyings, murders, drunkenness, revellings and such like: of the which I tell you before, as I have also told you in time past, that they which do such things shall not inherit the kingdom of God.

1 Corinthians 15:50 King James Version (KJV)
[50] Now this I say, brethren, that flesh and blood cannot inherit the kingdom of God; neither doth corruption inherit incorruption.

The scriptures above tell that **The Kingdom** is more than flesh and blood. It takes a reversal of Me, My and Mine. **The Kingdom** is spiritual because God is spiritual. Therefore, to achieve the spiritual we must work in the spiritual realm. This can only be accomplished when we are led by the transforming power of the Holy Spirit.

Before we pursue what is meant by "Spirit is born of spirit," let us identify what **The Kingdom of God** is. Scripture defines **The Kingdom** as **God's Kingdom**. When the scripture talks about a kingdom of someone, it is identifying that a certain individual is the ruler over a group of people or a nation. Therefore, when the scripture is talking of **God's Kingdom,** it is talking about a nation or a group of people under God's rule. Therefore, **The Kingdom** is a nation of people who are under the kingship of God, a nation of people who recognize Him as the ruler. They are a people who are under His authority and where He sets the rules and laws. He is the enforcer of the laws of His **Kingdom**. However, **God's Kingdom** is different from those of men on earth. In **God's Kingdom,** people voluntarily choose to follow God's rules and laws; they are not forced to as in earthly, man-led kingdoms. They choose to recognize that He is the true and only God, the creator of heaven and earth, not a mortal who makes a claim to be god or a person seeking to bring about his own glory. Therefore, when we become part of **The Kingdom of God,** God is our leader and His rules and laws take precedent over man's rules and laws. He does not need to puff Himself up or force us to follow Him. It is our choice whether we accept Him as King or not. When we recognize **Him** as our king and happily choose to follow His rules and laws and we choose to worship Him as the true God then we are participants in His Kingdom. So His kingdom is all that men's earthly kingdoms are not because we receive benefits in His kingdom that we cannot be found in earthly kingdoms. I will not go into all these here because the words I use will fall far short of describing these but the Holy Spirit can help you to understand this. The benefits of eternal life, love, joy, peace, fairness, no pain or suffering and happiness are just a few of these.

We become one with God and each other in **God's Kingdom**. The closest we have come to **The Kingdom** on earth other than Jesus the Christ himself was the first converts (The first 3,000 who were added on the day of Pentecost) to the church. Before this there was Enoch and his followers. Most of us usually say we cannot compare with Christ Jesus. Well maybe we can identify with the first 3,000 converts. Not only were these converted on Pentecost but the apostles and all those in the upper room were also. It took Enoch 360 years but on Pentecost, it occurred in one day. The details in scripture are very skimpy when it comes to Enoch. All we are told is that he pleased God and was translated (taken into God's dwelling).

Genesis 5:23-25 King James Version (KJV)
23 And all the days of Enoch were three hundred sixty and five years:
24 And Enoch walked with God: and he was not; for God took him.
25 And Methuselah lived an hundred eighty and seven years and begat Lamech.

In a matter of a few hours on the day of Pentecost there was a powerful move of the Holy Spirit and many repented and were converted. Here, on this day, the Holy Spirit transformed the spirit of man to a Godly spirit. In addition, I would like to point out something special that I believe about the first 3,000 converts. Not only did they experience a spiritual move in their lives many of these were probably among those who were witnesses of the risen Jesus the Christ. As scripture states, He appeared to 500 people after His resurrection and that the graves were opened the dead arose and went into Jerusalem. These too witnessed to people there. Their testimonies along with the testimony of Jesus convinced many of God's glory and His desire for us to follow him. Maybe they had been prepped in a special way for this day to occur. Meditate on the words of Paul below.

1 Corinthians 15:1-11 King James Version (KJV)
1 Moreover, brethren, I declare unto you the gospel which I preached unto you, which also ye have received and wherein ye stand;
2 By which also ye are saved, if ye keep in memory what I preached unto you, unless ye have believed in vain.
3 For I delivered unto you first of all that which I also received, how that Christ died for our sins according to the scriptures;
4 And that he was buried and that he rose again the third day according to the scriptures:
5 And that he was seen of Cephas, then of the twelve:
6 After that, he was seen of above five hundred brethren at once; of whom the greater part remain unto this present, but some are fallen asleep.
7 After that, he was seen of James; then of all the apostles.
8 And last of all he was seen of me also, as of one born out of due time.
9 For I am the least of the apostles, that am not meet to be called an apostle, because I persecuted the church of God.

[10] But by the grace of God I am what I am: and his grace which was bestowed upon me was not in vain; but I laboured more abundantly than they all: yet not I, but the grace of God which was with me.

[11] Therefore whether it were I or they, so we preach and so ye believed.

Matthew 27:47-54 *King James Version (KJV)*

[47] Some of them that stood there, when they heard that, said, This man calleth for Elias.

[48] And straightway one of them ran and took a spunge and filled it with vinegar and put it on a reed and gave him to drink.

[49] The rest said, Let be, let us see whether Elias will come to save him.

[50] Jesus, when he had cried again with a loud voice, yielded up the ghost.

[51] And, behold, the veil of the temple was rent in twain from the top to the bottom; and the earth did quake and the rocks rent;

[52] And the graves were opened; and many bodies of the saints which slept arose,

[53] And came out of the graves after his resurrection and went into the holy city and appeared unto many.

[54] Now when the centurion and they that were with him, watching Jesus, saw the earthquake and those things that were done, they feared greatly, saying, Truly this was the Son of God.

I am led to add a little more data on conversion. This is about how Jesus appeared to more than 500 people after His resurrection and those that were raised from the dead after His resurrection and went into Jerusalem and witnessed to many people. This to me is evidence of why many of the first 3,000 converts were so different from other converts who were added after Pentecost. They had seen the risen dead. They knew that life after death is real and that all they had been taught about God and His kingdom and knew it was true. So here, we have the preparation for the 3,000 that were added in one day. These people heard the scripture explained by the Holy Spirit and they humbled themselves and accepted His call to repentance. They accepted God's way as the only true way to live. Here on the day of Pentecost we see conversion or a rebirth take place. Nevertheless, after those first 3,000 converts, imperfection started to creep in.

Acts 2:1-24 King James Version (KJV)

[1] And when the day of Pentecost was fully come, they were all with one accord in one place.

[2] And suddenly there came a sound from heaven as of a rushing mighty wind and it filled all the house where they were sitting.

[3] And there appeared unto them cloven tongues like as of fire and it sat upon each of them.

[4] And they were all filled with the Holy Ghost and began to speak with other tongues, as the Spirit gave them utterance.

[5] And there were dwelling at Jerusalem Jews, devout men, out of every nation under heaven.

[6] Now when this was noised abroad, the multitude came together and were confounded, because that every man heard them speak in his own language.

[7] And they were all amazed and marvelled, saying one to another, Behold, are not all these which speak Galilaeans?

[8] And how hear we every man in our own tongue, wherein we were born?

[9] Parthians and Medes and Elamites and the dwellers in Mesopotamia and in Judaea and Cappadocia, in Pontus and Asia,

[10] Phrygia and Pamphylia, in Egypt and in the parts of Libya about Cyrene and strangers of Rome, Jews and proselytes,

[11] Cretes and Arabians, we do hear them speak in our tongues the wonderful works of God.

[12] And they were all amazed and were in doubt, saying one to another, What meaneth this?

[13] Others mocking said, These men are full of new wine.

[14] But Peter, standing up with the eleven, lifted up his voice and said unto them, Ye men of Judaea and all ye that dwell at Jerusalem, be this known unto you and hearken to my words:

[15] For these are not drunken, as ye suppose, seeing it is but the third hour of the day.

[16] But this is that which was spoken by the prophet Joel;

[17] And it shall come to pass in the last days, saith God, I will pour out of my Spirit upon all flesh: and your sons and your daughters shall prophesy and your young men shall see visions and your old men shall dream dreams:

[18] And on my servants and on my handmaidens I will pour out in those days of my Spirit; and they shall prophesy:

[19] And I will shew wonders in heaven above and signs in the earth beneath; blood and fire and vapour of smoke:

[20] The sun shall be turned into darkness and the moon into blood, before the great and notable day of the Lord come:

[21] And it shall come to pass, that whosoever shall call on the name of the Lord shall be saved.

[22] Ye men of Israel, hear these words; Jesus of Nazareth, a man approved of God among you by miracles and wonders and signs, which God did by him in the midst of you, as ye yourselves also know:

[23] Him, being delivered by the determinate counsel and foreknowledge of God, ye have taken and by wicked hands have crucified and slain:

[24] Whom God hath raised up, having loosed the pains of death: because it was not possible that he should be holden of it.

Acts 2:36-47 King James Version (KJV)
[36] Therefore let all the house of Israel know assuredly, that God hath made the same Jesus, whom ye have crucified, both Lord and Christ.

86

[37] Now when they heard this, they were pricked in their heart and said unto Peter and to the rest of the apostles, Men and brethren, what shall we do?

[38] Then Peter said unto them, Repent and be baptized every one of you in the name of Jesus Christ for the remission of sins and ye shall receive the gift of the Holy Ghost.

[39] For the promise is unto you and to your children and to all that are afar off, even as many as the Lord our God shall call.

[40] And with many other words did he testify and exhort, saying, Save yourselves from this untoward generation.

[41] Then they that gladly received his word were baptized: and the same day there were added unto them about three thousand souls.

[42] And they continued stedfastly in the apostles' doctrine and fellowship and in breaking of bread and in prayers.

[43] And fear came upon every soul: and many wonders and signs were done by the apostles.

[44] And all that believed were together and had all things common;

[45] And sold their possessions and goods and parted them to all men, as every man had need.

[46] And they, continuing daily with one accord in the temple and breaking bread from house to house, did eat their meat with gladness and singleness of heart,

[47] Praising God and having favour with all the people. And the Lord added to the church daily such as should be saved.

Not all the new converts have had the same preparation experiences as the initial 3,000. Therefore, they have not had the same conversion experiences. As we can see from this scripture, it takes a move of the Holy Spirit to convert us to be a part of His kingdom. When we are converted by this move of the Holy Spirit all things in our life and our perspective changes. It is no longer about Me, My and Mine. Our motives and desires are no longer driven by self-aggrandizement but by a desire to please God and to become one with God and our fellow brothers and sisters of God. When we are converted, we now emulate God's personality by choice and it is embedded in us. God has stated that He would place His Holy Spirit in man so that he would be able to abide in His kingdom and live a kingdom life.

Ezekiel 36:22-36 King James Version (KJV)

[22] Therefore say unto the house of Israel, thus saith the Lord God; I do not this for your sakes, O house of Israel, but for mine holy name's sake, which ye have profaned among the heathen, whither ye went.

[23] And I will sanctify my great name, which was profaned among the heathen, which ye have profaned in the midst of them; and the heathen shall know that

I am the Lord, saith the Lord God, when I shall be sanctified in you before their eyes.

24 For I will take you from among the heathen and gather you out of all countries and will bring you into your own land.

25 Then will I sprinkle clean water upon you and ye shall be clean: from all your filthiness and from all your idols, will I cleanse you.

26 A new heart also will I give you and a new spirit will I put within you: and I will take away the stony heart out of your flesh and I will give you an heart of flesh.

27 And I will put my spirit within you and cause you to walk in my statutes and ye shall keep my judgments and do them.

28 And ye shall dwell in the land that I gave to your fathers; and ye shall be my people and I will be your God.

29 I will also save you from all your uncleannesses: and I will call for the corn and will increase it and lay no famine upon you.

30 And I will multiply the fruit of the tree and the increase of the field, that ye shall receive no more reproach of famine among the heathen.

31 Then shall ye remember your own evil ways and your doings that were not good and shall lothe yourselves in your own sight for your iniquities and for your abominations.

32 Not for your sakes do I this, saith the Lord God, be it known unto you: be ashamed and confounded for your own ways, O house of Israel.

33 Thus saith the Lord God; In the day that I shall have cleansed you from all your iniquities I will also cause you to dwell in the cities and the wastes shall be builded.

34 And the desolate land shall be tilled, whereas it lay desolate in the sight of all that passed by.

35 And they shall say, This land that was desolate is become like the garden of Eden; and the waste and desolate and ruined cities are become fenced and are inhabited.

36 Then the heathen that are left round about you shall know that I the Lord build the ruined places and plant that that was desolate: I the Lord have spoken it and I will do it.

So, these first 3,000 people on the day of Pentecost were not only living in this world but they were also endued with God's Holy Spirit, which enabled them to seek and communicate with the spirit. Herein the Holy Spirit was generating spiritual things in the spirit of man. They became a people who lived to please God and who lived with the love of God in their heart and emulated His ways. They became a people whose heart and goals were like His. They became one with Him. So those in God's kingdom are those who are like Him and live their lives as he intended from the beginning. That is why the first 3,000 converts were able to shun the desire to own material goods. They gave them up and sold them because they were no longer important for them as individuals. God provided it for the establishment of His Kingdom.

Like many, my conversion has been a slow on-going process and it has taken many years for God to bring me to this point. Like many of you I still have those problem areas in my life which I am not proud of. God is continually working to change these in my life. Praise him for His patience and grace.

There is one aspect of God's kingdom I am led to point out using the example of the first 3,000 converts. A difference can be seen in how they chose to live their lives. The first 3,000 people added to the church considered none of their property as their own. They recognized that God is the source and owner of everything, so they shared all things and there was no poor among them. Because they willingly shared in their provisions, everyone received provision as he had need. Note, this was not based on equality but based on each one's needs. Some needed more, but some needed less. No one was hoarding or seeking to have more for the sake of selfishness. This was a direct result of having been converted by the Holy Spirit of God; they became one with God and with each other. God was attempting to demonstrate this in the providing of manna to the people of Israel when they left Egypt. No one lacked and God provided each person according to their need not according to their desires.

Exodus 16:15-22 King James Version (KJV)

[15] And when the children of Israel saw it, they said one to another, It is manna: for they wist not what it was. And Moses said unto them, This is the bread which the Lord hath given you to eat.

[16] This is the thing which the Lord hath commanded, Gather of it every man according to his eating, an omer for every man, according to the number of your persons; take ye every man for them which are in his tents.

[17] And the children of Israel did so and gathered, some more, some less.

[18] And when they did mete it with an omer, he that gathered much had nothing over and he that gathered little had no lack; they gathered every man according to his eating.

[19] And Moses said, Let no man leave of it till the morning.

[20] Notwithstanding they hearkened not unto Moses; but some of them left of it until the morning and it bred worms and stank: and Moses was wroth with them.

[21] And they gathered it every morning, every man according to his eating: and when the sun waxed hot, it melted.
[22] And it came to pass, that on the sixth day they gathered twice as much bread, two omers for one man: and all the rulers of the congregation came and told Moses.

One true indicator of God's kingdom is that those who obtain to it are in it will consider and love their brethren just as themselves. They will recognize that all things are God's, not ours and are to be shared to meet everyone's individual needs. That is, we will share in God's abundance as God intends for each of us.

As we see in the scripture in Acts the second chapter, when we repent in response to the prompting of the Holy Spirit and are baptized in accordance with God's choice, we receive the Holy Spirit in our baptism. Repentance is more than mere words. We recognize that we have not lived in accordance with God's rules and that everything about us needs to be reborn spiritually (converted). Only after this, can God endue us with the full power of His Holy Spirit, which is the only way **The Kingdom** can be established.

God said, "Let us create man in our own image", which in the beginning, was to enable man to be one in spirit and likeness with God's ways and thinking. God did not want to force us to be like Him, so He allowed us to have the right to choose, just like the angels, whether we would accept His ways.

Genesis 1:21-23 King James Version (KJV)
[21] And God created great whales and every living creature that moveth, which the waters brought forth abundantly, after their kind and every winged fowl after his kind: and God saw that it was good.
[22] And God blessed them, saying, Be fruitful and multiply and fill the waters in the seas and let fowl multiply in the earth.
[23] And the evening and the morning were the fifth day.

Genesis 1:25-27 King James Version (KJV)
[25] And God made the beast of the earth after his kind and cattle after their kind and every thing that creepeth upon the earth after his kind: and God saw that it was good.
[26] And God said, Let us make man in our image, after our likeness: and let them have dominion over the fish of the sea and over the fowl of the air and over the cattle and over all the earth and over every creeping thing that creepeth upon the earth.

27 So God created man in his own image, in the image of God created he him; male and female created he them.

Genesis 4:11-13 - Inspired Version

11 And Eve, his wife, heard all these things and was glad, saying, Were it not for our transgression, we never should have known good and evil and the joy of our redemption and the eternal life which God giveth unto all the obedient.
12 And Adam and Eve blessed the name of God; and they made all things known unto their sons and daughters.
13 And Satan came among them, saying, I am also a son of God and he commanded them, saying, Believe it not. And they believed it not; and they loved Satan more than God. And men began from that time forth to be carnal, sensual and devilish.

SUMMARY

God has provided guidelines to show what it takes for us to live our lives as He originally intended, in His image, which is spiritual. He has provided a method for that to be accomplished. Jesus has provided us with salvation so that we might have a clean slate by which we can build a new relationship with God so that our spirit can be aligned the way God intended from the beginning. He has allowed us to make choices until we come to recognize that His ways are best. God allows us to learn by the choices we make while living in our fleshly lusts and desires. He also states that everyone has within him a conscience that will cause him to know both right and wrong. So, no one is exempt from being able to choose what is right and wrong as we all have a method by which we judge ourselves. Therefore, when we fully accept Jesus and we are converted by His Spirit, then **God's Kingdom** arrives.

The following passages indicate that **The Kingdom** or Zion is no farther away than our spiritual condition justifies. When we look at scripture, there is a brief reference about how God took up Enoch without death because he pleased God. Enoch was a man who pleased God because he lived life the way God intended. Not just in word but by deed and in spirit also. This is the same relationship we need to develop for God to be pleased with us.

Doctrine and Covenants section 6:3a -63b

[Sec 6:3a] Now, as you have asked, behold, I say unto you, Keep my commandments and seek to bring forth and establish the cause of Zion:

[Sec 6:3b] seek not for riches but for wisdom; and, behold, the mysteries of God shall be unfolded unto you and then shall you be made rich.

Hebrews 11:5-6 King James Version (KJV)

[5] By faith Enoch was translated that he should not see death; and was not found, because God had translated him: for before his translation he had this testimony, that he pleased God.
[6] But without faith it is impossible to please him: for he that cometh to God must believe that he is and that he is a rewarder of them that diligently seek him.

Doctrine and Covenants section 36:2h-36:3b

[Sec 36:2h] And the Lord called his people Zion, because they were of one heart and one mind and dwelt in righteousness;
[Sec 36:2i] and there was no poor among them; and Enoch continued his preaching in righteousness unto the people of God.
[Sec 36:3a] And it came to pass in his days that he built a city that was called the city of holiness, even ZION.
[Sec 36:3b] And it came to pass that Enoch talked with the Lord and he said unto the Lord, Surely Zion shall dwell in safety forever.

Doctrine and Covenants section 140:5c

[Sec 140:5c] The work of preparation and the perfection of my Saints go forward slowly and Zionic conditions are no further away nor any closer than the spiritual condition of my people justifies;

Finally:

2 Chronicles 7:14

[14] if my people who are called by my name humble themselves, pray, seek my face and turn from their wicked ways, then I will hear from heaven and will forgive their sin and heal their land.

We need to humble ourselves, look at how we are making choices and repent, asking God to bring about a transformation in our spirit that will cause us to be about building His kingdom and not about looking after self, so that we can live here on earth, just as in heaven. When we begin to walk in the spirit and allow the Holy Spirit to help us become one in Him and with each other, then we will consider all that we do. We will do all for God's glory, not ours. Then spirit will bring about spirit and God's Kingdom will be here on earth.

CHAPTER 8

Hunger And Thirst After Righteousness

The formula here is

RT = M X C²

Where

RT = Righteousness

M = Man

C² = Christ Multiplied by the Comforter (the Holy Spirit)

The equation here is that for man to achieve righteous behavior requires a work of the Holy Spirit. Jesus the Christ left the Holy Spirit to help us to learn and choose to emulate the Character of God himself (to be what he wanted when were created in His image), so that we can live in God's presence.

Genesis 1:26-28 King James Version (KJV)
[26] And God said, Let us make man in our image, after our likeness: and let them have dominion over the fish of the sea and over the fowl of the air and over the cattle and over all the earth and over every creeping thing that creepeth upon the earth.
[27] So God created man in his own image, in the image of God created he him; male and female created he them.
[28] And God blessed them and God said unto them, Be fruitful and multiply and replenish the earth and subdue it: and have dominion over the fish of the sea and over the fowl of the air and over every living thing that moveth upon the earth.

God cannot tolerate sin, nor will he allow it in heaven. So, for us to be in condition for Christ Jesus to return, He wants the same conditions here on earth as it is in heaven (the Lord's Prayer). God's goal is to prove that good will overcome evil. That is demonstrated when man accepts God's ways as the best and is willing to allow God to change his ways to be the same as His. Then we will be in His likeness and will walk in righteousness.

The Spirit will reveal to us areas in our lives that are not consistent with God's character. This may require a complete remake of us in certain areas (voluntary change implemented by the Holy Spirit), an act which only God can perform (we cannot will it to be so or force it or do it on our own nor will God force it upon us). Scripture says all have sinned and fallen short of the glory of God.

Romans 3:23:19-26 King James Version (KJV)

[19] Now we know that what things soever the law saith, it saith to them who are under the law: that every mouth may be stopped and all the world may become guilty before God.

[20] Therefore by the deeds of the law there shall no flesh be justified in his sight: for by the law is the knowledge of sin.

[21] But now the righteousness of God without the law is manifested, being witnessed by the law and the prophets;

[22] Even the righteousness of God which is by faith of Jesus Christ unto all and upon all them that believe: for there is no difference:

[23] For all have sinned and come short of the glory of God;

[24] Being justified freely by his grace through the redemption that is in Christ Jesus:

[25] Whom God hath set forth to be a propitiation through faith in his blood, to declare his righteousness for the remission of sins that are past, through the forbearance of God;

[26] To declare, I say, at this time his righteousness: that he might be just and the justifier of him which believeth in Jesus.

Most of us try to mask or hide our behavioral flaws (pockets of sinful thoughts or behavior) from others and at times we even hide them from ourselves. Remember that which is born of the flesh is flesh and that which is born of the spirit is spirit.

John 3:5-7 King James Version (KJV)

[5] Jesus answered, Verily, verily, I say unto thee, Except a man be born of water and of the Spirit, he cannot enter into the kingdom of God.

[6] That which is born of the flesh is flesh; and that which is born of the Spirit is spirit.

[7] Marvel not that I said unto thee, Ye must be born again.

Romans 8:4-6 King James Version (KJV)

[4] That the righteousness of the law might be fulfilled in us, who walk not after the flesh, but after the Spirit.

[5] For they that are after the flesh do mind the things of the flesh; but they that are after the Spirit the things of the Spirit.

[6] For to be carnally minded is death; but to be spiritually minded is life and peace.

When we accept the invitation to accept Christ through baptism, even though we say we have repented of all sin, we need a spiritual transformation for true repentance to occur. God wants us to be changed (transformed) in spirit. Baptism is just the first step in our transformation. It is like opening a doorway for spiritual transformation. Spiritual transformation can only take place when he reveals the iniquity, unrighteousness and sin in our innermost self to us.

When we recognize that those particular areas in our lives are out of step with His and are willing to allow Him to change these. Then He will be able to bestow within us His righteousness. If we do not want to change, He will not force us to change. But, as He reveals these areas of sin in our life, we need to be open to allowing the Holy Spirit to modify these areas so that we can choose to emulate God's choices and His ways. Thus, by allowing our choices to be the same as His our righteous will match His. This does not destroy our individuality, but enhances it. God's objective is to have a people here on earth that are the same as the people in heaven, so that others will see the benefit it brings to this world and desire to be the same. So, when we desire to have God transform us to a righteous people (hunger and thirst after righteousness), then he can transform us into His likeness. Righteousness is about the motives for doing good deeds, not just about doing good deeds for the sake of doing good deeds. Scripture states that doing good works without the Spirit of God behind it and without the glory of God as a goal is worthless in God's site. Many do good works out of a sense of duty or responsibility and not the heartfelt love that God has for each individual.

Matthew 5:1-7 King James Version (KJV)

[1] And seeing the multitudes, he went up into a mountain: and when he was set, his disciples came unto him:
[2] And he opened his mouth and taught them, saying,
[3] Blessed are the poor in spirit: for theirs is the kingdom of heaven.
[4] Blessed are they that mourn: for they shall be comforted.
[5] Blessed are the meek: for they shall inherit the earth.
[6] Blessed are they which do hunger and thirst after righteousness: for they shall be filled.
[7] Blessed are the merciful: for they shall obtain mercy.

Righteousness should be a goal for us. I keep using the word goal because most of us have them, even though we do not recognize them as such. We strive for many things in life, fun, happiness and riches, comfort and so on and so forth. Scripture says we should hunger for (strive to achieve) righteousness. This is more than an intellectual assent. It takes a conversion of our motives to be the same as God's motives. Scripture is pointing out that this is not a natural state for us as humans. It states that for the most part, we are carnal. Carnal meaning our goals, actions and our character are based on fleshly lusts that are selfish in most areas. See the following scripture:

Genesis 8:21 King James Version (KJV)
[21] And the Lord smelled a sweet savour; and the Lord said in his heart, I will not again curse the ground any more for man's sake; for the imagination of man's heart is evil from his youth; neither will I again smite any more every thing living, as I have done.

Philippians 3:17-19 King James Version (KJV)
[17] Brethren, be followers together of me and mark them which walk so as ye have us for an ensample.
[18] (For many walk, of whom I have told you often and now tell you even weeping, that they are the enemies of the cross of Christ:
[19] Whose end is destruction, whose God is their belly and whose glory is in their shame, who mind earthly things.)

So, what is righteousness? According to the insight I have received, it is living in accordance with God's principles or to have our character emulate or be like God or Christ Jesus. God's character as stated in scripture is:

Numbers 23:19 King James Version (KJV)
[19] God is not a man, that he should lie; neither the son of man, that he should repent: hath he said and shall he not do it? or hath he spoken and shall he not make it good?

Deuteronomy 4:31 King James Version (KJV)
[31] (For the <u>Lord thy God is a merciful God;</u>) he will not forsake thee, neither destroy thee, nor forget the covenant of thy fathers which he sware unto them.

Deuteronomy 7:9 King James Version (KJV)
[9] Know therefore that the <u>Lord thy God, he is God, the faithful God, which keepeth covenant and mercy with them that love him and keep his commandments to a thousand generations;</u>

Deuteronomy 10:17 King James Version (KJV)
[17] For the Lord your <u>God is God of gods and Lord of lords, a great God, a mighty and a terrible, which regardeth not persons, nor taketh reward:</u>

2 Chronicles 30:9 King James Version (KJV)
[9] For if ye turn again unto the Lord, your brethren and your children shall find compassion before them that lead them captive, so that they shall come again into this land: for the <u>Lord your God is gracious and merciful</u> and will not turn away his face from you, if ye return unto him.

Job 36:5 King James Version (KJV)
[5] Behold, <u>God is mighty and despiseth not any: he is mighty in strength and wisdom.</u>

Job 36:22 King James Version (KJV)
[22] Behold, <u>God exalteth by his power: who teacheth like him?</u>

Psalm 7:11 King James Version (KJV)
[11] <u>God judgeth the righteous and God is angry with the wicked every day.</u>

Psalm 46:1 King James Version (KJV)
[1] <u>God is our refuge and strength, a very present help in trouble.</u>

Psalm 54:4 King James Version (KJV)
[4] Behold, <u>God is mine helper</u>: the Lord is with them that uphold my soul.

Psalm 116:5 King James Version (KJV)
[5] <u>Gracious is the Lord and righteous; yea, our God is merciful.</u>

John 3:33 King James Version (KJV)
[33] He that hath received his testimony hath set to his seal that <u>God is true.</u>

1 Corinthians 1:9 King James Version (KJV)
[9] <u>God is faithful,</u> by whom ye were called unto the fellowship of his Son Jesus Christ our Lord.

1 Corinthians 14:33 King James Version (KJV)
[33] For <u>God is not the author of confusion, but of peace,</u> as in all churches of the saints.

1 John 4:8 King James Version (KJV)
[8] He that loveth not knoweth not God; for <u>God is love.</u>

Exodus 34:6 King James Version (KJV)
[6] And the Lord passed by before him and proclaimed, <u>The Lord, The Lord God, merciful and gracious, longsuffering and abundant in goodness and truth,</u>

The above scriptures tell us some of God's characteristics. Scripture also tells us in the words of Jesus the Christ that if we have seen Jesus, then we have seen, in His life, God. This is because in all that He did, He did in accordance with God's character. Jesus stated that He did not do anything unless He first saw the Father do it. He was the embodiment of God here on earth in that the things he did were performed in the same manner and with the same motives as the Father.

John 14:8-10 King James Version (KJV)
[8] Philip saith unto him, Lord, show us the Father and it sufficeth us.
[9] Jesus saith unto him, Have I been so long time with you and yet hast thou not known me, Philip? he that hath seen me hath seen the Father; and how sayest thou then, Show us the Father?
[10] Believest thou not that I am in the Father and the Father in me? the words that I speak unto you I speak not of myself: but the Father that dwelleth in me, he doeth the works.

Since we are not in the Father's presence, we need to use the scripture, aided by the Holy Spirit, to lead us into learning God's ways and who he is. If we intently study the character of Jesus, then we will learn the true attributes of God.

The following scripture combines most of the above and identifies God's righteous behavior as fruits of the Spirit. It also gives us insight into works of the flesh.

Galatians 5:13-26 King James Version (KJV)
[13] For, brethren, ye have been called unto liberty; only use not liberty for an occasion to the flesh, but by love serve one another.
[14] For all the law is fulfilled in one word, even in this; Thou shalt love thy neighbour as thyself.
[15] But if ye bite and devour one another, take heed that ye be not consumed one of another.
[16] This I say then, Walk in the Spirit and ye shall not fulfil the lust of the flesh.
[17] For the flesh lusteth against the Spirit and the Spirit against the flesh: and these are contrary the one to the other: so that ye cannot do the things that ye would.
[18] But if ye be led of the Spirit, ye are not under the law.
[19] Now the works of the flesh are manifest, which are these; Adultery, fornication, uncleanness, lasciviousness,
[20] Idolatry, witchcraft, hatred, variance, emulations, wrath, strife, seditions, heresies,

²¹ Envyings, murders, drunkenness, revellings and such like: of the which I tell you before, as I have also told you in time past, that they which do such things shall not inherit the kingdom of God.

²² But the fruit of the Spirit is love, joy, peace, longsuffering, gentleness, goodness, faith,

²³ Meekness, temperance: against such there is no law.

²⁴ And they that are Christ's have crucified the flesh with the affections and lusts.

²⁵ If we live in the Spirit, let us also walk in the Spirit.

²⁶ Let us not be desirous of vain glory, provoking one another, envying one another.

I recognize it has taken a long time for me to understand that it takes a work of the Holy Spirit in my life for me to want to change and allow the Holy Spirit to make changes in the parts of my character that are not in alignment with those God wants in my life. I will point out a couple of flaws (iniquity) in my character that I knew were working against my being as God desired me to be. So here it goes:

I have always had a feeling of being a failure and not being successful. Even though God has provided me with many talents and skills, I have always felt like I fell short of being the best that I could be. More pointedly, I wanted to be better than everyone else was. Well, when God called me to the ministry I really wanted to succeed at this. So, I started studying and preaching. The problem was I was preaching *at* people rather than calling them to repentance and teaching them to live a life like the one God wants. I would yell and scream at the congregation trying to show how sinful they were. Yes, I was truly a fire and brimstone preacher. Then the Holy Spirit helped me to notice, slowly but surely, that my attitude was all wrong and rather than preaching to condemn people, I should be teaching them in love to accept God and the benefits of living the way He desires. So, God started making a change in my attitude toward His children. This was evidenced one day after I had said the communion prayers. Afterward, a member of our congregation came up and asked what had happened to me! She said that when I said those prayers, she could feel the love of God in them rather than the usual condemning way I had been saying them. This was accomplished by the work of the Holy Spirit when he caused me to realize that the way I was doing things was not right. When I came to the point of wanting to change my ways, the Holy Spirit was able to work with my spirit to make this change in me.

Another instance was early in my relationship with my mother in-law. I had an on-going dislike for her and this is putting it mildly. When I received the call to be an Evangelist, I knew this needed to change for me to be able to minister properly in my calling. So, I began praying to God to change this feeling within me. One day when she was coming for her annual summer visit to see my wife and our children, we went to pick her up at the airport. In a single moment in time, something miraculous happened. All of a sudden when I saw her coming down the walkway from the plane, something came over me in a way I cannot put into words. But simultaneously, our hearts melted and from then on I loved her as a son is supposed to love his mother. After that, we had a wonderful relationship and had the greatest of joy being in each other's company. This is also putting it mildly.

Next, I would like to point out the problem with my temper. I have always had a bad temper and have known that I needed to have this changed for me to be more the way God wants me to be. I try to mask this around others, so only those who are very close to me know about this. I prayed repeatedly for God to make this change in me. Then one day he answered! He told me in audible words that He could not take this away from me because I like to be angry. Wow, what a revelation that was! Slowly, I began to realize God would not go against our will. Even though he has been able to take the edge off my temper, He still has not been able to completely remove it, since there is some reason I keep holding on to this aspect of my character.

I have learned that if there is an area of sinful attitude or behavior in our life that we place off limits to God, He will not go there. Even though I know that this needs to change in my life, He cannot transform this sin to a righteous attitude until I allow Him to. I realize that Moses had a similar issue with anger.

Numbers 20:6-12 King James Version (KJV)

⁶ And Moses and Aaron went from the presence of the assembly unto the door of the tabernacle of the congregation and they fell upon their faces: and the glory of the Lord appeared unto them.

⁷ And the Lord spake unto Moses, saying,

⁸ Take the rod and gather thou the assembly together, thou and Aaron thy brother and speak ye unto the rock before their eyes; and it shall give forth his water and thou shalt bring forth to them water out of the rock: so thou shalt give the congregation and their beasts drink.

⁹ And Moses took the rod from before the Lord, as he commanded him.

¹⁰ And Moses and Aaron gathered the congregation together before the rock and he said unto them, Hear now, ye rebels; must we fetch you water out of this rock?

¹¹ And Moses lifted up his hand and with his rod he smote the rock twice: and the water came out abundantly and the congregation drank and their beasts also.

¹² And the Lord spake unto Moses and Aaron, Because ye believed me not, to sanctify me in the eyes of the children of Israel, therefore ye shall not bring this congregation into the land which I have given them.

As you can see in the above scripture, Moses in anger struck the rock. He was told to speak to the rock so that God would be glorified. For this act, Moses was not allowed to enter the Promised Land.

Therefore, I guess this is a lesson for us all. We need to ask Him to expose to us those areas in our character where we need to allow him to make changes in order to be righteous. We need to ask Him how to release the source of these issues, so that we can allow him, through the Holy Spirit to transform these areas to His holy and righteous ways. That conversation with God about my anger opened my understanding to the fact that each of us has deeply embedded in our subconscious many things that we have hidden from ourselves. We may not have an understanding or knowledge of the cause or reasoning for them, but God does.

Romans 8:28-30 King James Version (KJV)

²⁸ And we know that all things work together for good to them that love God, to them who are the called according to his purpose.

²⁹ For whom he did foreknow, he also did predestinate to be conformed to the image of his Son, that he might be the firstborn among many brethren.

³⁰ Moreover whom he did predestinate, them he also called: and whom he called, them he also justified: and whom he justified, them he also glorified.

So, we have a Holy Spirit, who was provided to help us to conform to the image of Christ Jesus so that when He returns, we will know Him because we will be like Him (made in His image). Scripture tells us not to resist the Holy Spirit so that he can perform the things he was sent to perform.

Ephesians 4:29-31 King James Version (KJV)

[29] Let no corrupt communication proceed out of your mouth, but that which is good to the use of edifying, that it may minister grace unto the hearers.
[30] And grieve not the holy Spirit of God, whereby ye are sealed unto the day of redemption.
[31] Let all bitterness and wrath and anger and clamour and evil speaking, be put away from you, with all malice:

Being righteous requires us to actively allow the Holy Spirit of God to work in us through prayer, study and fasting. He can then perform the same marvelous work that he has done in others, so that we can be like Him. To become a people who please Him, so that we can be in His presence. I can tell you that like Paul, I am not yet perfect, but I strive for the call to be like Jesus the Christ. For some, this process is easy, but for those like me, it is like pulling teeth, a tough long process. I guess the same might be said of Enoch. He succeeded, but it took 360 years before he truly pleased God. It does not have to take that long for you and I if we will only submit to the Holy Spirit and truly want to be the way God calls us to be. I guess you can call this an ongoing goal for each of us or the way to the cross and truly walking in the Spirit.

We need a spiritual rejuvenation that for most will require a renewal of the spirit through what we term as spiritual cleansing with the help of those who understand the spiritual requirements for this process. This is done through us being led to a point where the spirit is able to bring a healing to our spirit and release us from past roadblocks we have established to God's ministry. For some this can be done in one session. for others, it takes more. This is what occurred on the day of Pentecost in the upper room and with the first 3,000 converts to the church. It started with the appearance of the resurrected dead who came forth on the day of Jesus's resurrection and was completed on the day of Pentecost.

I end with this:

James 4:8 King James Version (KJV)
[8] Draw nigh to God and he will draw nigh to you. Cleanse your hands, ye sinners; and purify your hearts, ye double minded.

Or in modern day language:

James 4:8 Amplified Bible (AMP)
8 Come close to God [with a contrite heart] and He will come close to you. Wash your hands, you sinners; and purify your [unfaithful] hearts, you double-minded [people].

These words were written to those in the church as well as those without.

CHAPTER 9

Merciful Shall Get Mercy

Matthew 5:7 King James Version (KJV)
[7] Blessed are the merciful: for they shall obtain mercy.

Luke 6:36 King James Version (KJV)
[36] Be ye therefore merciful, as your Father also is merciful.

The Formula here is

> **ME = M x C²**
>
> **Where**
>
> **ME symbolizes for Mercy**
>
> **M is Man**
>
> **C² is Christ times the Comforter**

Most would interpret the scripture above to mean that if we are merciful to all men, then men will be merciful to us. Do you remember the famous phrase we all are familiar with, "Do unto others as you would have them do unto you?" However, this scripture does not say that because we show mercy to others they will return the favor. This, as all of us know, is not the case because those with an evil heart and intentions will not always respond in a positive manner.

Matthew 12:34-36 King James Version (KJV)
[34] O generation of vipers, how can ye, being evil, speak good things? for out of the abundance of the heart the mouth speaketh.

[35] A good man out of the good treasure of the heart bringeth forth good things: and an evil man out of the evil treasure bringeth forth evil things.

[36] But I say unto you, That every idle word that men shall speak, they shall give account thereof in the day of judgment.

Luke 6:45 King James Version (KJV)

[45] A good man out of the good treasure of his heart bringeth forth that which is good; and an evil man out of the evil treasure of his heart bringeth forth that which is evil: for of the abundance of the heart his mouth speaketh.

Romans 12:6-21 King James Version (KJV)

[6] Having then gifts differing according to the grace that is given to us, whether prophecy, let us prophesy according to the proportion of faith;

[7] Or ministry, let us wait on our ministering: or he that teacheth, on teaching;

[8] Or he that exhorteth, on exhortation: he that giveth, let him do it with simplicity; he that ruleth, with diligence; he that sheweth mercy, with cheerfulness.

[9] Let love be without dissimulation. Abhor that which is evil; cleave to that which is good.

[10] Be kindly affectioned one to another with brotherly love; in honour preferring one another;

[11] Not slothful in business; fervent in spirit; serving the Lord;

[12] Rejoicing in hope; patient in tribulation; continuing instant in prayer;

[13] Distributing to the necessity of saints; given to hospitality.

[14] Bless them which persecute you: bless and curse not.

[15] Rejoice with them that do rejoice and weep with them that weep.

[16] Be of the same mind one toward another. Mind not high things, but condescend to men of low estate. Be not wise in your own conceits.

[17] Recompense to no man evil for evil. Provide things honest in the sight of all men.

[18] If it be possible, as much as lieth in you, live peaceably with all men.

[19] Dearly beloved, avenge not yourselves, but rather give place unto wrath: for it is written, Vengeance is mine; I will repay, saith the Lord.

[20] Therefore if thine enemy hunger, feed him; if he thirst, give him drink: for in so doing thou shalt heap coals of fire on his head.

[21] Be not overcome of evil, but overcome evil with good.

Here what scripture is telling us is to emulate God's mercy to all because God shows mercy to us out of His love. As has been stated before, scripture tells us the heart of man is evil continually. Therefore, without a spiritual transformation we cannot attain the goal of being merciful.

Jesus used the parable of the Good Samaritan to demonstrate this.

Luke 10:25-37 King James Version (KJV)

[25] And, behold, a certain lawyer stood up and tempted him, saying, Master, what shall I do to inherit eternal life?

²⁶ He said unto him, What is written in the law? how readest thou?

²⁷ And he answering said, Thou shalt love the Lord thy God with all thy heart and with all thy soul and with all thy strength and with all thy mind; and thy neighbour as thyself.

²⁸ And he said unto him, Thou hast answered right: this do and thou shalt live.

²⁹ But he, willing to justify himself, said unto Jesus, And who is my neighbour?

³⁰ And Jesus answering said, A certain man went down from Jerusalem to Jericho and fell among thieves, which stripped him of his raiment and wounded him and departed, leaving him half dead.

³¹ And by chance there came down a certain priest that way: and when he saw him, he passed by on the other side.

³² And likewise a Levite, when he was at the place, came and looked on him and passed by on the other side.

³³ But a certain Samaritan, as he journeyed, came where he was: and when he saw him, he had compassion on him,

³⁴ And went to him and bound up his wounds, pouring in oil and wine and set him on his own beast and brought him to an inn and took care of him.

³⁵ And on the morrow when he departed, he took out two pence and gave them to the host and said unto him, Take care of him; and whatsoever thou spendest more, when I come again, I will repay thee.

³⁶ Which now of these three, thinkest thou, was neighbour unto him that fell among the thieves?

³⁷ And he said, He that shewed mercy on him. Then said Jesus unto him, Go and do thou likewise.

The Samaritan in the parable demonstrates what happens when we are open to letting the Holy Spirit work in our lives. The Samaritan was influenced by the love of God and his receptiveness to the Holy Spirit. That receptiveness allowed the Holy Spirit to cause him to love the man enough to be merciful. The religious leaders excused their conduct in this parable. They demonstrated what happens when we are not receptive and open to the guidance of the Holy Spirit. We are more prone to follow man's fleshly desires rather than God's righteousness. It also demonstrates that a hard heart does not change just because of the label we place on ourselves. Evil is evil whether we profess to follow God or not.

I have experienced similar situations in modern day times. I will use an example of an incident I witnessed quite often. There was a pastor of a big, fancy and very popular church in the neighborhood where I grew up. I would see him driving to church in his big, empty Cadillac every week. He would routinely pass up little old ladies on canes who were barely able to walk. He would wave, honk and then pass them up. Now, I am not saying he was a bad person, but I am saying that his heart was hardened in an area that prevented him from being receptive to the promptings of the Holy Spirit to be merciful. (Needless to say, this turned me against this denomination, but looking back, I cannot say I was any better at the time). Just claiming to be religious, sounding religious, or looking religious is not enough to demonstrate we will adhere to the tenets of God's gospel. This is a common problem in the church now. We claim to be Christians, but we have decided to live in accordance to what is acceptable to us. We follow societal norms and selfish motives; not what God calls us to follow. Just as the nation of Israel, God's chosen people, we live in accordance with our own lusts and pleasures, picking and choosing which tenets of the gospel we will adhere to and how we want to interpret the gospel. God is clear about what He calls us to be and how we are to live our lives. However, because we have not been converted (or are not following the guidance of the Holy Spirit), we seek our own ways using our own understanding and not following the Holy Spirit's guidance.

Our ability to be merciful depends on our obedience to the guidance of the Holy Spirit and the daily repentance we are to practice. For most of us this a difficult task to perform because we are used to following our own way. For some, this comes naturally because God has given them attribute as an example to us all. As the entire gospel demonstrates, we need to humble ourselves and repent and ask God to rejuvenate us and convert us to His ways. Conversion only comes as we submit to the Holy Spirit and are willing to allow God's ways to be our ways. Refer to chapter 8. This is what God says we have to have to renew our minds, which can only occur through the work of Holy Spirit. King David understood this and so did Paul.

Psalm 51:9-11 King James Version (KJV)
[9] Hide thy face from my sins and blot out all mine iniquities.
[10] Create in me a clean heart, O God; and renew a right spirit within me.
[11] Cast me not away from thy presence; and take not thy holy spirit from me.

Romans 12:1-3 King James Version (KJV)

[1] I beseech you therefore, brethren, by the mercies of God, that ye present your bodies a living sacrifice, holy, acceptable unto God, which is your reasonable service.

[2] And be not conformed to this world: but be ye transformed by the renewing of your mind, that ye may prove what is that good and acceptable and perfect, will of God.

[3] For I say, through the grace given unto me, to every man that is among you, not to think of himself more highly than he ought to think; but to think soberly, according as God hath dealt to every man the measure of faith.

Ephesians 4:22-24 King James Version (KJV)

[22] That ye put off concerning the former conversation the old man, which is corrupt according to the deceitful lusts;

[23] And be renewed in the spirit of your mind;

[24] And that ye put on the new man, which after God is created in righteousness and true holiness.

Titus 3:4-6 King James Version (KJV)

[4] But after that the kindness and love of God our Saviour toward man appeared,

[5] Not by works of righteousness which we have done, but according to his mercy he saved us, by the washing of regeneration and renewing of the Holy Ghost;

[6] Which he shed on us abundantly through Jesus Christ our Saviour;

CHAPTER 10

True Peace On Earth As It Is In Heaven

Matthew 5:9 King James Version (KJV)
[9] Blessed are the peacemakers: for they shall be called the children of God.

The formula here is:

$$TP = M \times C^2$$

Where:

TP = True Peace

M = Man

C^2 = Christ multiplied by the Comforter (the Holy Spirit)

The equation here is that true peace (TP) can only be obtained when the Holy Spirit in conjunction with Jesus the Christ (C2) transforms our choices to act in the principles of God (His righteousness and love). Peace has to start in us individually. Then God can bring peace through us.

Who are the peacemakers and why is it they are different from the rest of the world? Well let us look at the ones we hold in high esteem. For the most part, it is those who are the great warriors. Mention Genghis Khan and we all recognize him. Why not consider Patton or Hitler? On the other hand, should I also mention our sport's heroes? The only reason we recognize men like Lincoln or George Washington, is because they fought for a cause to obtain peace through force. The Bible says blessed are the peacemakers. People like Gandhi or Martin Luther King or Sister Teresa, those who fought evil with peaceful actions, are seen as being weak. Most people hate someone who they see as weak. God wants a world with peaceful coexistence but ever since Cain and Able there has been enmity between God and man. For man seeks to establish his way by force not through the ways of peace. God seeks to establish His Kingdom through a cooperative effort. So, if we do things God's way he will support our efforts but if we do things our way then God leaves us to the results of our own choices.

True Peace can only be established under God's terms. When we can express love to God and love to our neighbors and when we are able to be one with one another as God, Jesus the Christ and the Holy Spirit are one with one another, then and only then can peace come to us. A condition of peace exists when we seek the good of our brother and ourselves out of love for them and God. The purpose should be to establishing a situation where no one seeks to harm anyone else and we work together in harmony (love) by choice, not by force. Peace is an internal condition that can only be established by the power of the Holy Spirit working within us. The conditions of peace can only exist when the conditions of the kingdom of God exist because it can only be established through the work of God. It is something that starts in us individually in our spirit voluntarily, not by force.

Luke 17:19-21 King James Version (KJV)
[19] And he said unto him, Arise, go thy way: thy faith hath made thee whole.
[20] And when he was demanded of the Pharisees, when the kingdom of God should come, he answered them and said, The kingdom of God cometh not with observation:
[21] Neither shall they say, Lo here! or, lo there! for, behold, the kingdom of God is within you.

Matthew 11:11-15 King James Version (KJV)
[11] Verily I say unto you, Among them that are born of women there hath not risen a greater than John the Baptist: notwithstanding he that is least in the kingdom of heaven is greater than he.
[12] And from the days of John the Baptist until now the kingdom of heaven suffereth violence and the violent take it by force.
[13] For all the prophets and the law prophesied until John.
[14] And if ye will receive it, this is Elias, which was for to come.
[15] He that hath ears to hear, let him hear.

So how do we arrive at the point that brings us to be a peace-loving people who seek the common good under God's rule? There have been many who have tried to set up cults, which claim to be peaceful communities. Some claim they are even led by God, but they fall far short of what God wants. First, peace has to be something that is born from within from the right motives and principles. Many of the so-called peaceful cults have failed for the same reasons: either they leave God out, or they are following man's ways, trying to force the conditions they have identified which exemplify peace. Without humbling ourselves and seeking true repentance and having God establish His righteousness in us, we cannot succeed in finding and establishing true peace. No matter what we try to do, our attempts will be futile without God's guidance. We see peace as absence of war. However, it is much more than that. Scripture tells us this in many ways.

Romans 5:1-3 King James Version (KJV)
5 Therefore being justified by faith, we have peace with God through our Lord Jesus Christ:
² By whom also we have access by faith into this grace wherein we stand and rejoice in hope of the glory of God.
³ And not only so, but we glory in tribulations also: knowing that tribulation worketh patience;

Philippians 4:4-9 King James Version (KJV)
⁴ Rejoice in the Lord always: and again I say, Rejoice.
⁵ Let your moderation be known unto all men. The Lord is at hand.
⁶ Be careful for nothing; but in every thing by prayer and supplication with thanksgiving let your requests be made known unto God.
⁷ And the peace of God, which passeth all understanding, shall keep your hearts and minds through Christ Jesus.
⁸ Finally, brethren, whatsoever things are true, whatsoever things are honest, whatsoever things are just, whatsoever things are pure, whatsoever things are lovely, whatsoever things are of good report; if there be any virtue and if there be any praise, think on these things.
⁹ Those things, which ye have both learned and received and heard and seen in me, do: and the God of peace shall be with you.

Colossians 3:14-16 King James Version (KJV)
¹⁴ And above all these things put on charity, which is the bond of perfectness.
¹⁵ And let the peace of God rule in your hearts, to the which also ye are called in one body; and be ye thankful.
¹⁶ Let the word of Christ dwell in you richly in all wisdom; teaching and admonishing one another in psalms and hymns and spiritual songs, singing with grace in your hearts to the Lord.

See how the at the time of the building of the tower of Babel there were a people of one accord or the number of times Israel was told not to make peace treaties with other nations.

In our denomination, we have those who offer daily prayers for peace, but peace has yet to arrive. Why is this? Until people submit fully to God, there cannot be true peace. Peace is an inner trait not an outward look. Without the transforming of the Holy Spirit man cannot achieve true or lasting peace. Remember, God will not go against man's agency. Unless we are willing to allow this change to occur in us, it will not. Scripture states that peace will not return to the earth until Jesus returns.

Early in the establishment of the Church of Jesus Christ, as it was called at that time, the prophet tried to establish what God had called for - a peaceful community, but it failed. Why? One reason was that the people established a militia for protection. The only protection God's people need is God and His angel armies. So, when we take up arms to protect ourselves, are we seeking peace? In the early days of the nation of Israel, God tried to get them to allow him to fight their battles, but they wanted to defend themselves. Why? They did not really trust God to do this for them. Are we any different? We have a vast nuclear arsenal but is there world peace or even peace in our land?

Deuteronomy 1:29-31 King James Version (KJV)
[29] Then I said unto you, Dread not, neither be afraid of them.
[30] The Lord your God which goeth before you, he shall fight for you, according to all that he did for you in Egypt before your eyes;
[31] And in the wilderness, where thou hast seen how that the Lord thy God bare thee, as a man doth bear his son, in all the way that ye went, until ye came into this place.

The early church formed after Pentecost was a peaceful group. They allowed themselves to be tortured and allowed themselves to be killed for the sake of establishing a nation under God. Then, as many who were not truly transformed came into the church, fear also came.

I cannot hold myself in any greater esteem than any of the above. Case in point:

Many people in our church saw me as a peace-loving, kind-hearted man. A situation occurred one day while I was attending one of our church camps as a youth counselor. At a basketball game one of the other counselors was being assaulting one of the referees. He was also a church member and much larger in stature than the referee. It was easy to see one person as the aggressor and the other as the one who was only trying to fend off a much stronger opponent. Reluctantly, I took it upon myself to try to bring about a peaceful resolution and help the weaker of the two who really was not able to withstand the big bully. I stood between the two and tried to get the bully to calm down. The aggressor in this situation turned and threatened me! My anger flared up and I was ready to fight! Several others came and had to pull us apart. This showed how peaceful I was. Put in the right situation, most of us will respond in the same way. Here you can see I responded in the flesh, not in the Holy Spirit. I thought because I was a minister in God's church I could diffuse the situation in my own strength but I was wrong. In order for peace to prevail, I needed to be filled and fully transformed by the Holy Spirit, which had not occurred at that point. I was trying to be the person of God I was called to be, but I had not attained-the fullness of transformation God needed to have done in me. I realize now God allowed this situation to happen to teach me more of Him. Fortunately, for the three of us, God was able to bring others to defuse this situation to stop any further harm from occurring.

The way of true peace is demonstrated in scripture in the Book of Mormon where it describes a group of men who had taken a vow to not take up a sword against another man. When their enemy attacked them, they fell to their knees and allowed themselves to be killed without any resistance, saying they were honoring their vow to God. The enemy kept attacking and after the battle, some were converted because they saw the love of God at work. Note, not all the others responded to the peaceful acts of these men, only those whose hearts would allow the Holy Spirit to touch them. Sometimes we have to suffer to allow the Holy Spirit to bring about the repentance of others. We have been accustomed to looking for our earthly leaders to protect us because we do not trust God to do it. We are told he has legions galore to protect us, but we do not trust this, so we take up arms to protect ourselves. We need to ask God for the ability to see into the spirit realm so that we can see His legions of angel armies for ourselves.

In Leviticus, God made a promise to the people of Israel that if they would follow all His ways he would protect them and they would have peace in their land. However, they did not follow His ways, so their enemies overran them because God let them suffer the results of their choices.

Leviticus 26:1-11 King James Version (KJV)
[1] Ye shall make you no idols nor graven image, neither rear you up a standing image, neither shall ye set up any image of stone in your land, to bow down unto it: for I am the Lord your God.
[2] Ye shall keep my sabbaths and reverence my sanctuary: I am the Lord.
[3] If ye walk in my statutes and keep my commandments and do them;
[4] Then I will give you rain in due season and the land shall yield her increase and the trees of the field shall yield their fruit.
[5] And your threshing shall reach unto the vintage and the vintage shall reach unto the sowing time: and ye shall eat your bread to the full and dwell in your land safely.
[6] And I will give peace in the land and ye shall lie down and none shall make you afraid: and I will rid evil beasts out of the land, neither shall the sword go through your land.
[7] And ye shall chase your enemies and they shall fall before you by the sword.
[8] And five of you shall chase an hundred and an hundred of you shall put ten thousand to flight: and your enemies shall fall before you by the sword.
[9] For I will have respect unto you and make you fruitful and multiply you and establish my covenant with you.
[10] And ye shall eat old store and bring forth the old because of the new.
[11] And I set my tabernacle among you: and my soul shall not abhor you.

So here, we see that for true peace to be established it will require a people who are willing to follow God's tenets and trust Him to be true to His promises. God instructed Moses to have His priests to say a blessing over the people whenever they met, but because of the hardness of their hearts, they refused the influence of the Holy Spirit and the blessing did not cause them to pursue the ways of peace.

Numbers 6:22-24 King James Version (KJV)
[22] And the Lord spake unto Moses, saying,
[23] Speak unto Aaron and unto his sons, saying, On this wise ye shall bless the children of Israel, saying unto them,
[24] The Lord bless thee and keep thee:
[25] The Lord make his face shine upon thee and be gracious unto thee:
[26] The Lord lift up his countenance upon thee and give thee peace.
[27] And they shall put my name upon the children of Israel and I will bless them.
 Judges 6:24 King James Version (KJV)
[24] Then Gideon built an altar there unto the Lord and called it Jehovahshalom[1]: unto this day it is yet in Ophrah of the Abiezrites.

Here we can see God has always wanted us to be at peace but that peace comes at a price and can only be established through him. The work of peace

---

[1] This is translated Jehovah send peace.

can only come when people submit to the Holy Spirit (the countenance of God) to work. We must be willing to follow His commandments and submit to Him. This only comes by allowing the Holy Spirit to bring a transformation in us to be a loving righteous people. Only then can we be a people who can turn the other cheek, show love to our enemy or be able to say and be truthful with the words, "Forgive them for they know not what they do." As can be seen by my testimony above, my spiritual transformation had not reached the point to respond in a Godly manner. Therefore, I responded to the fiery situation with anger and without Holy righteousness.

Matthew 5:39 King James Version (KJV)
³⁹ But I say unto you, That ye resist not evil: but whosoever shall smite thee on thy right cheek, turn to him the other also.

Luke 23:34 King James Version (KJV)
³⁴ Then said Jesus, Father, forgive them; for they know not what they do. And they parted his raiment and cast lots.

Acts 7:54-60 King James Version (KJV)
⁵⁴ When they heard these things, they were cut to the heart and they gnashed on him with their teeth.
⁵⁵ But he, being full of the Holy Ghost, looked up stedfastly into heaven and saw the glory of God and Jesus standing on the right hand of God,
⁵⁶ And said, Behold, I see the heavens opened and the Son of man standing on the right hand of God.
⁵⁷ Then they cried out with a loud voice, and stopped their ears, and ran upon him with one accord,
⁵⁸ And cast him out of the city and stoned him: and the witnesses laid down their clothes at a young man's feet, whose name was Saul.
⁵⁹ And they stoned Stephen, calling upon God and saying, Lord Jesus, receive my spirit.
⁶⁰ And he kneeled down and cried with a loud voice, Lord, lay not this sin to their charge. And when he had said this, he fell asleep.

Acts 8:1-4 King James Version (KJV)
¹ And Saul was consenting unto his death. And at that time there was a great persecution against the church which was at Jerusalem; and they were all scattered abroad throughout the regions of Judaea and Samaria, except the apostles.
² And devout men carried Stephen to his burial and made great lamentation over him.
³ As for Saul, he made havock of the church, entering into every house and haling men and women committed them to prison.
⁴ Therefore they that were scattered abroad went every where preaching the word.

117

Only when we are filled with the Holy Spirit as Stephen was can we be at peace within ourselves and with our enemies. It takes a transformed people who have been filled with the righteousness of God to be able to practice true peace because with true peace there has to be a Godly love embedded in us. World peace will only come when Jesus returns. Until then we have to pursue peace in the inward person.

Zechariah 14:3-5 King James Version (KJV)

³ Then shall the Lord go forth and fight against those nations, as when he fought in the day of battle.

⁴ And his feet shall stand in that day upon the mount of Olives, which is before Jerusalem on the east and the mount of Olives shall cleave in the midst thereof toward the east and toward the west and there shall be a very great valley; and half of the mountain shall remove toward the north and half of it toward the south.

⁵ And ye shall flee to the valley of the mountains; for the valley of the mountains shall reach unto Azal: yea, ye shall flee, like as ye fled from before the earthquake in the days of Uzziah king of Judah: and the Lord my God shall come and all the saints with thee.

Revelation 20:1-15 King James Version (KJV)

¹ And I saw an angel come down from heaven, having the key of the bottomless pit and a great chain in his hand.

² And he laid hold on the dragon, that old serpent, which is the Devil and Satan and bound him a thousand years,

³ And cast him into the bottomless pit and shut him up and set a seal upon him, that he should deceive the nations no more, till the thousand years should be fulfilled: and after that he must be loosed a little season.

⁴ And I saw thrones and they sat upon them and judgment was given unto them: and I saw the souls of them that were beheaded for the witness of Jesus and for the word of God and which had not worshipped the beast, neither his image, neither had received his mark upon their foreheads, or in their hands; and they lived and reigned with Christ a thousand years.

⁵ But the rest of the dead lived not again until the thousand years were finished. This is the first resurrection.

⁶ Blessed and holy is he that hath part in the first resurrection: on such the second death hath no power, but they shall be priests of God and of Christ and shall reign with him a thousand years.

⁷ And when the thousand years are expired, Satan shall be loosed out of his prison,

⁸ And shall go out to deceive the nations which are in the four quarters of the earth, Gog and Magog, to gather them together to battle: the number of whom is as the sand of the sea.

⁹ And they went up on the breadth of the earth and compassed the camp of the saints about and the beloved city: and fire came down from God out of heaven and devoured them.

[10] And the devil that deceived them was cast into the lake of fire and brimstone, where the beast and the false prophet are and shall be tormented day and night for ever and ever.

[11] And I saw a great white throne and him that sat on it, from whose face the earth and the heaven fled away; and there was found no place for them.

[12] And I saw the dead, small and great, stand before God; and the books were opened: and another book was opened, which is the book of life: and the dead were judged out of those things which were written in the books, according to their works.

[13] And the sea gave up the dead which were in it; and death and hell delivered up the dead which were in them: and they were judged every man according to their works.

[14] And death and hell were cast into the lake of fire. This is the second death.

[15] And whosoever was not found written in the book of life was cast into the lake of fire.

CHAPTER 11

Persecuted Shall Receive Great Reward In Heaven

Judges 2:18 King James Version (KJV)
[18] And when the Lord raised them up judges, then the Lord was with the judge and delivered them out of the hand of their enemies all the days of the judge: for it repented the Lord because of their groanings by reason of them that oppressed them and vexed them.

Matthew 5:10 King James Version (KJV)
[10] Blessed are they which are persecuted for righteousness' sake: for theirs is the kingdom of heaven.

Galatians 4:29 King James Version (KJV)
[29] But as then he that was born after the flesh persecuted him that was born after the Spirit, even so it is now.

2 Timothy 3:12 King James Version (KJV)
[12] Yea and all that will live godly in Christ Jesus shall suffer persecution.

Hebrews 11:32-40 King James Version (KJV)
[32] And what shall I more say? for the time would fail me to tell of Gedeon and of Barak and of Samson and of Jephthae; of David also and Samuel and of the prophets:
[33] Who through faith subdued kingdoms, wrought righteousness, obtained promises, stopped the mouths of lions.
[34] Quenched the violence of fire, escaped the edge of the sword, out of weakness were made strong, waxed valiant in fight, turned to flight the armies of the aliens.
[35] Women received their dead raised to life again: and others were tortured, not accepting deliverance; that they might obtain a better resurrection:
[36] And others had trial of cruel mockings and scourgings, yea, moreover of bonds and imprisonment:
[37] They were stoned, they were sawn asunder, were tempted, were slain with the sword: they wandered about in sheepskins and goatskins; being destitute, afflicted, tormented;

[38] (Of whom the world was not worthy:) they wandered in deserts and in mountains and in dens and caves of the earth.

[39] And these all, having obtained a good report through faith, received not the promise:

[40] God having provided some better thing for us, that they without us should not be made perfect.

The formula here is

$$PF = M \times C^2$$

Where:

PF = Perfection

M = Man

C^2 = Christ multiplied by the Comforter (the Holy Spirit)

Where PF stands for the perfection of all saints and as before M = man and C^2 = The Comforter X Christ

Since we are to be one in Christ, the perfection of the saints is to be one (united). Until all who are in the Lamb's book of life are together in heaven, Jesus's full work, though His work on earth is complete, is incomplete. Each of us are called to be one in Christ Jesus and if one of us suffers, we all suffer. When one of us reaches perfection we all reach perfection.

Ephesians 4:12-14 King James Version (KJV)
[12] For the perfecting of the saints, for the work of the ministry, for the edifying of the body of Christ:
[13] Till we all come in the unity of the faith and of the knowledge of the Son of God, unto a perfect man, unto the measure of the stature of the fulness of Christ:
[14] That we henceforth be no more children, tossed to and fro and carried about with every wind of doctrine, by the sleight of men and cunning craftiness, whereby they lie in wait to deceive;

Hebrews 11:39-40 King James Version (KJV)
[39] And these all, having obtained a good report through faith, received not the promise:
[40] God having provided some better thing for us, that they without us should not be made perfect.

We have to do this as individuals, but until the total work is done in all of us the work of Jesus cannot be completed. That is one reason He is constantly interceding on our behalf.

Hebrews 7:25 King James Version (KJV)

²⁵ Wherefore he is able also to save them to the uttermost that come unto God by him, seeing he ever liveth to make intercession for them.

So, we have Jesus and the Holy Spirit who are working on behalf of all who desire to be one with Him because just as he was persecuted, so we shall be. Just as He was able to withstand persecution through the power of the Holy Spirit, which is the love of God spread abroad in our hearts, through that same power we can also withstand persecution. Persecution requires a strength that most of us do not possess without the Spirit of God in us. It is an attack on our spirit, not just bodily suffering. We hear of bodily suffering in modern day times in countries far away. Persecution also takes place in our country. Hence, we are reluctant in many ways to admit we are Christians and to walk in the ways God has outlined.

I recall many times when I was reluctant to admit that I was a Christian. I would in many ways avoid telling people that I believed in Jesus Christ by word and deed. I did not want to be seen as a holy roller or Jesus freak. When it came to saying out loud that I believed I would avoid it by trying to duplicate the behavior of those around me. This is because I wanted to be acceptable to most men. Through the years I have grown to regret those choices. But now after many years the Spirit of God has transformed my spirit so that now I am willing to publicly display my Christian beliefs. I am not yet perfect but eagerly await that transformation.

Genesis 17:1-3 King James Version (KJV)
¹ And when Abram was ninety years old and nine, the Lord appeared to Abram and said unto him, I am the Almighty God; walk before me and be thou perfect.
² And I will make my covenant between me and thee and will multiply thee exceedingly.
³ And Abram fell on his face: and God talked with him, saying,

Deuteronomy 18:12-14 King James Version (KJV)
¹² For all that do these things are an abomination unto the Lord: and because of these abominations the Lord thy God doth drive them out from before thee.
¹³ Thou shalt be perfect with the Lord thy God.
¹⁴ For these nations, which thou shalt possess, hearkened unto observers of times and unto diviners: but as for thee, the Lord thy God hath not suffered thee so to do.

2 Chronicles 16:8-10 King James Version (KJV)
⁸ Were not the Ethiopians and the Lubims a huge host, with very many chariots and horsemen? yet, because thou didst rely on the Lord, he delivered them into thine hand.

[9] For the eyes of the Lord run to and fro throughout the whole earth, to shew himself strong in the behalf of them whose heart is perfect toward him. Herein thou hast done foolishly: therefore from henceforth thou shalt have wars.

[10] Then Asa was wroth with the seer and put him in a prison house; for he was in a rage with him because of this thing. And Asa oppressed some of the people the same time.

Matthew 5:48 King James Version (KJV)

[48] Be ye therefore perfect, even as your Father which is in heaven is perfect.

Early in my Christian walk I did not like to listen to Christian music on the radio. I enjoyed the music I grew up listening to, Motown. One day the Holy Spirit helped me to realize that the words in the secular music were causing me to think the wrong things. So, I decided to try listening to a Christian radio station. It was not easy at first, but the Holy Spirit caused my opinion to change. Slowly but surely my thoughts started turning more to God instead of those fleshly thoughts which secular music was reinforcing. I now enjoy listening to Christian music on the radio and love those songs which praise God. I have learned that not all so-called Christian songs are about God. Many Christian artists believe the only way to make money is by appealing to the secular crowd as well as Christian believers. They write music which does not mention God and try to use words that will appeal to those who do not know God. Now there are some Christian songs that are more about the flesh than the spirit, but there are many that are about God and His righteousness. The Holy Spirit helps me to delight in these and many times I wake with these songs being replayed in my mind. They uplift my spirit and turn my heart more and more toward him.

I used to be ashamed to say a blessing over food when eating in public. One day the Holy Spirit caused me to know this was wrong. So, I started saying blessings in public, but in a prideful way. I then was moved by the Holy Spirit to make these prayers be prayers of thanks to God. Not something for show, but something between me and Him even though it was in public.

I realize that in comparison to some of the things that the early Christians endured, this is persecution on an extremely low level. But it is still a form of persecution, one that impaired my walk with God and kept me from growing in Him for a time. I no longer worry about what people may think, say, or do to me as a result of being and acting like a Christian. As true Christians, we cannot be more concerned with the persecution or ridicule of Man than who God wants us to be.

124

I could point out numerous times where the Holy Spirit has caused changes to be made in my spirit, but I believe from the few I have mentioned, you are starting to get the point. Hopefully, you can not only see my issues, but also the steps of repentance that took place and how the Holy Spirit has been able to transform me to new levels of God's righteousness. He transforms not only my behavior, but my spiritual outlook to purpose not to follow the fleshly norms, but to walk in His love.

I am no longer a closet Christian. I enjoy the fact that now I feel free to express my belief in God no matter where I am.

I could mention the persecution which Christians are experiencing in many other countries but most Americans cannot identify with this.

The scripture which the Lord points us to is

Matthew 19:26 King James Version (KJV)
²⁶ But Jesus beheld them and said unto them, With men this is impossible; but with God all things are possible.

And also

Philippians 4:13 King James Version (KJV)
¹³ I can do all things through Christ which strengtheneth me.

This is how the first 3,000, who became the start of the Christian church (and many others) were able to endure persecution. This is how those today who undergo persecution endure it. Enabled by the Holy Spirit with the strength and resolve of Christ Jesus, we can endure persecution because we have His love and power implanted in our spirit.

From this I see we are all one in Christ. When we attain this point of conversion, we are able to do the work God called us to do, which is to be a light on the hill. Not that we will receive the benefits here on earth in earthly terms, but we will be able to celebrate that all who are willing will be one with us in heaven and on earth.

We are called to allow Jesus to be seen through us by those He has called to be with Him, so that the kingdom building work can proceed in the manner God has ordained. We are called to emulate Christ Jesus in every way. Even in the face of persecution.

Zechariah 8:23 King James Version (KJV)

[23] Thus saith the Lord of hosts; In those days it shall come to pass, that ten men shall take hold out of all languages of the nations, even shall take hold of the skirt of him that is a Jew, saying, We will go with you: for we have heard that God is with you.

CHAPTER 12

Let Your Light Shine With Good Works To Glorify Your Father In Heaven

Matthew 5:16 King James Version (KJV)
[16] Let your light so shine before men, that they may see your good works and glorify your Father which is in heaven.

Acts 9:36 King James Version (KJV)
[36] Now there was at Joppa a certain disciple named Tabitha, which by interpretation is called Dorcas: this woman was full of good works and almsdeeds which she did.

1 Timothy 5:10 King James Version (KJV)
[10] Well reported of for good works; if she have brought up children, if she have lodged strangers, if she have washed the saints' feet, if she have relieved the afflicted, if she have diligently followed every good work.

1 Timothy 5:24-25 King James Version (KJV)
[24] Some men's sins are open beforehand, going before to judgment; and some men they follow after.
[25] Likewise also the good works of some are manifest beforehand; and they that are otherwise cannot be hid.

Titus 2:7 King James Version (KJV)
[7] In all things shewing thyself a pattern of good works: in doctrine shewing uncorruptness, gravity, sincerity,

Titus 3:1-8 King James Version (KJV)
[1] Put them in mind to be subject to principalities and powers, to obey magistrates, to be ready to every good work,
[2] To speak evil of no man, to be no brawlers, but gentle, shewing all meekness unto all men.

³ For we ourselves also were sometimes foolish, disobedient, deceived, serving divers lusts and pleasures, living in malice and envy, hateful and hating one another.
⁴ But after that the kindness and love of God our Saviour toward man appeared,
⁵ Not by works of righteousness which we have done, but according to his mercy he saved us, by the washing of regeneration and renewing of the Holy Ghost;
⁶ Which he shed on us abundantly through Jesus Christ our Saviour;
⁷ That being justified by his grace, we should be made heirs according to the hope of eternal life.
⁸ This is a faithful saying and these things I will that thou affirm constantly, that they which have believed in God might be careful to maintain good works. These things are good and profitable unto men.

Titus 3:14 King James Version (KJV)
¹⁴ And let our's also learn to maintain good works for necessary uses, that they be not unfruitful.

The formula here is

$$TGW = M \times C^2$$

Where:

TGW = True Good Works

M = Man

C^2 = Christ magnified by the Comforter (the Holy Spirit)

That is TGW is true good works is created in us through the work of the Comforter (the Holy Spirit) and Christ Jesus.

As stated before, true good works are those that proceed out the heart, not just the good deeds done for the sake of good deeds in the flesh. We all know some people who are truly kind hearted and who do good works. In scripture Dorcas was one such person. She was constantly doing good deeds and people recognized something special in the way she performed her good works. It was not just what she did, but the way in which it was done. The reason behind her deeds. Everyone recognized that what she did was uniquely special. There was a quality of love apparent in each thing she did and it was this that made her so precious to others. Sure, there were others doing good works, but what she did stood out to everyone. Why? It was the spirit behind what she did that everyone admired. It was the transforming work of the Holy Spirit which was made evident in why she did what she did, rather than the act itself.

Acts 9:36-42 King James Version (KJV)
³⁶ Now there was at Joppa a certain disciple named Tabitha, which by interpretation is called Dorcas: this woman was full of good works and almsdeeds which she did.

³⁷ And it came to pass in those days, that she was sick and died: whom when they had washed, they laid her in an upper chamber.

³⁸ And forasmuch as Lydda was nigh to Joppa and the disciples had heard that Peter was there, they sent unto him two men, desiring him that he would not delay to come to them.

³⁹ Then Peter arose and went with them. When he was come, they brought him into the upper chamber: and all the widows stood by him weeping and shewing the coats and garments which Dorcas made, while she was with them.

⁴⁰ But Peter put them all forth and kneeled down and prayed; and turning him to the body said, Tabitha, arise. And she opened her eyes: and when she saw Peter, she sat up.

⁴¹ And he gave her his hand and lifted her up and when he had called the saints and widows, presented her alive.

⁴² And it was known throughout all Joppa; and many believed in the Lord.

So as in all works of the Holy Spirit, we find that it is more than the doing that counts. It is a true transformation of motives that matters. This can be pointed out with the acts of Mary and Martha in scripture. Martha did the work that needed to be done because it was her duty to do so. She did what she did because it was expected of her and she had been taught this, but something was missing. There was no joy in doing it, only the sense of responsibility. See the following quote from scripture:

Luke 10:38-42 King James Version (KJV)
³⁸ Now it came to pass, as they went, that he entered into a certain village: and a certain woman named Martha received him into her house.
³⁹ And she had a sister called Mary, which also sat at Jesus' feet and heard his word.
⁴⁰ But Martha was cumbered about much serving and came to him and said, Lord, dost thou not care that my sister hath left me to serve alone? bid her therefore that she help me.
⁴¹ And Jesus answered and said unto her, Martha, Martha, thou art careful and troubled about many things:
⁴² But one thing is needful: and Mary hath chosen that good part, which shall not be taken away from her.

In the scripture above Martha is upset because Mary is not taking part in the work that needed to be done. But Jesus pointed out that Mary was participating in something more needful, the transforming of her spirit. Martha was doing a good work but her heart was not in it. Her motive was duty not the love the Holy Spirit can place in your heart so that you have joy in doing good works. That is the element that is lacking in many who try to do good works. Case in point:

There was a young lady who was a member of the church who wanted to get more involved in doing some good works. It was Christmas time and the Salvation Army was looking for volunteers to help distribute toys. She volunteered. On one of her deliveries, there was this family who had several kids and who were very poor. There were several new toys scattered in the yard. When the young lady brought more toys and the family did not show any gratitude, the young lady became very angry and she let them know it. When she came back to church, she stated volunteering had been the worst experience of her life and that she would not take part in anything like that again because people are so ungrateful. Whose sin was the greatest, hers or those who were poor and very likely not members of any church. The young lady had not been converted to the point that she could bear such incidents, so she was not equipped to handle such matters yet. Just as is stated in scripture, the spirit was willing but the flesh was weak. Here was a tremendous opportunity for her to have been a great witness but she let the flesh rule instead of the Holy Spirit. She had not come to the point where He could make this transformation in her spirit yet. Now I don't condemn her because I am not sure I would have done any differently. I just know the Holy Spirit was able to let me understand the error of her ways. It was a teaching point for me.

There is a common movement that we hear of in the church today. This movement is to establish men as the head of the household but promotes that they should "rule" their household. So many men today are trying to force their family to obey everything they say (a dictatorship). That is not the way Christ rules the church. First, He allows us to learn His ways, not by force but by choice, and His example and through His teaching. He does not force us to do anything. If we want to do wrong, then He will allow us to do so and will also allow us to suffer the consequences. Only when we are willing to respond in love will he help us to walk in His ways. Note the word help, not force. Christ is not a dictator. His ways are not our ways. We cannot emulate His ways without the work of the Holy Spirit converting us to His ways and that only occurs when we are willing for it to happen.

I will point out an example of this. One day I was getting my car serviced and this gentleman was talking to his wife on the phone. I did not know the situation, but he was trying to force her into doing something the way he wanted. He kept saying, very forcefully I may add, that scripture said he was the head of the family and that she needed to submit to him! It became apparent that she finally hung up while he was in mid-sentence of stating he was the God appointed head of the household. Evidently, she did not comply with his demands nor did she see him as the head of the household.

The thing that we need to get into our guts is that when we do good works out of duty or self-aggrandizement or to make ourselves feel good, then we working in the flesh. As in all the works of God, we need to learn to work in love, which has been transplanted in us by the Holy Spirit. Otherwise, we cannot please God. Pleasing God should be the motive behind all that we do as a Christian. When we identify (or when the Holy Spirit causes us to identify) we are working in the wrong way, we should repent and ask God to have the Holy Spirit rejuvenate us to work in His righteousness. So many today do many good things for the wrong reasons. We have been instructed to pray before we undertake anything. And that prayer should be that the love of God be the master of what we are about to do [and that we do it] through the transforming work of the Holy Spirit.

Hebrews 13:17-19 King James Version (KJV)
[17] Obey them that have the rule over you and submit yourselves: for they watch for your souls, as they that must give account, that they may do it with joy and not with grief: for that is unprofitable for you.
[18] Pray for us: for we trust we have a good conscience, in all things willing to live honestly.
[19] But I beseech you the rather to do this, that I may be restored to you the sooner.

Matthew 7:22-24 King James Version (KJV)
[22] Many will say to me in that day, Lord, Lord, have we not prophesied in thy name? and in thy name have cast out devils? and in thy name done many wonderful works?
[23] And then will I profess unto them, I never knew you: depart from me, ye that work iniquity.
[24] Therefore whosoever heareth these sayings of mine and doeth them, I will liken him unto a wise man, which built his house upon a rock:

Philippians 4:6 King James Version (KJV)
[6] Be careful for nothing; but in every thing by prayer and supplication with thanksgiving let your requests be made known unto God.

Proverbs 3:5-6 King James Version (KJV)
[5] Trust in the Lord with all thine heart; and lean not unto thine own understanding.
[6] In all thy ways acknowledge him and he shall direct thy paths.

1 John 5:14 King James Version (KJV)

[14] And this is the confidence that we have in him, that, if we ask any thing according to his will, he heareth us:

CHAPTER 13

Take Up Your Cross Be Humble

2 Corinthians 12:20 King James Version (KJV)
20 For I fear, lest, when I come, I shall not find you such as I would and that I shall be found unto you such as ye would not: lest there be debates, envyings, wraths, strifes, backbitings, whisperings, swellings, tumults:

Luke 18:9-14 King James Version (KJV)
9 And he spake this parable unto certain which trusted in themselves that they were righteous and despised others:
10 Two men went up into the temple to pray; the one a Pharisee and the other a publican.
11 The Pharisee stood and prayed thus with himself, God, I thank thee, that I am not as other men are, extortioners, unjust, adulterers, or even as this publican.
12 I fast twice in the week, I give tithes of all that I possess.
13 And the publican, standing afar off, would not lift up so much as his eyes unto heaven, but smote upon his breast, saying, God be merciful to me a sinner.
14 I tell you, this man went down to his house justified rather than the other: for every one that exalteth himself shall be abased; and he that humbleth himself shall be exalted.

Luke 18:18-23 King James Version (KJV)
18 And a certain ruler asked him, saying, Good Master, what shall I do to inherit eternal life?
19 And Jesus said unto him, Why callest thou me good? none is good, save one, that is, God.
20 Thou knowest the commandments, Do not commit adultery, Do not kill, Do not steal, Do not bear false witness, Honour thy father and thy mother.
21 And he said, All these have I kept from my youth up.
22 Now when Jesus heard these things, he said unto him, Yet lackest thou one thing: sell all that thou hast and distribute unto the poor and thou shalt have treasure in heaven: and come, follow me.
23 And when he heard this, he was very sorrowful: for he was very rich.

The Formula here is:

$$HUM = MC^2$$

Where

HUM = Humble yourself to follow the cross

M = Man

C^2 = the saving grace of Christ Jesus multiplied by the Comforter (Holy Spirit)

Taking up one's cross has to do with removing those things in our lives which go against the works of God. This is wrapped up in the phrases self-righteousness or self-aggrandizement. It is the way we consider those things which are a benefit for ourselves only, without regard for others. It is a selfish walk whereby we set ourselves at odds with others by elevating ourselves, condemning others, or by considering them less than ourselves and not worthy. Just as the scripture above pointed out, there is much bickering, jealousy, anger, strife, backbiting, envy, gossip, disagreements and tumult in the church today. We see these as the reasons many churches split or just die today.

Selfish behaviors can be expressed in the church and in life in many forms. One example is greed. This occurs when we chose to believe that God intends for us to be wealthier or better off than our brothers and sisters because we deserve it. Again, this is a self-righteous expression. We consider ourselves more worthy than others and so consider ourselves to be more deserving. So, we hoard God's provisions just as the rich ruler above so that we can be assured we can take care of ourselves and our comfort at the expense of others. We consider that we deserve as much as we can get. We all feel we own the property we have and that it is for us and us only. We worked for it, so it belongs to us, right? We miss the point that the earth is the Lord's and the fullness thereof!

Deuteronomy 10:13-15 King James Version (KJV)
[13] To keep the commandments of the Lord and his statutes, which I command thee this day for thy good?
[14] Behold, the heaven and the heaven of heavens is the Lord's thy God, the earth also, with all that therein is.

[15] Only the Lord had a delight in thy fathers to love them and he chose their seed after them, even you above all people, as it is this day.

Luke 12:13-21 King James Version (KJV)

[13] And one of the company said unto him, Master, speak to my brother, that he divide the inheritance with me.

[14] And he said unto him, Man, who made me a judge or a divider over you?

[15] And he said unto them, Take heed and beware of covetousness: for a man's life consisteth not in the abundance of the things which he possesseth.

[16] And he spake a parable unto them, saying, The ground of a certain rich man brought forth plentifully:

[17] And he thought within himself, saying, What shall I do, because I have no room where to bestow my fruits?

[18] And he said, This will I do: I will pull down my barns and build greater; and there will I bestow all my fruits and my goods.

[19] And I will say to my soul, Soul, thou hast much goods laid up for many years; take thine ease, eat, drink and be merry.

[20] But God said unto him, Thou fool, this night thy soul shall be required of thee: then whose shall those things be, which thou hast provided?

[21] So is he that layeth up treasure for himself and is not rich toward God.

Acts 2:44-46 King James Version (KJV)

[44] And all that believed were together and had all things common;

[45] And sold their possessions and goods and parted them to all men, as every man had need.

[46] And they, continuing daily with one accord in the temple and breaking bread from house to house, did eat their meat with gladness and singleness of heart,

1 Corinthians 10:25-27 King James Version (KJV)

[25] Whatsoever is sold in the shambles, that eat, asking no question for conscience sake:

[26] For the earth is the Lord's and the fulness thereof.

[27] If any of them that believe not bid you to a feast and ye be disposed to go; whatsoever is set before you, eat, asking no question for conscience sake.

Another selfish behavior is pride. We all like to consider ourselves to either be better than others, or we consider ourselves to be worthless, or somewhere in between. All are expressions of pride. At one end of the spectrum is an exalted pride and at the other end is a wounded one. Neither one allows you to be considered in the light God intended for you when he created you. These are as much a sin as murder or stealing. We were all created equal in God's sight, so anything that is used to express anything other than that is far short of what he intended. The only reason God cannot accept us is because of our choice to sin. It is not people God is intolerant of, it is sin. Scripture says we are all made worthy through the sacrifice of Jesus the Christ of Nazareth.

135

Jesus himself used the example of humbling himself to the position of the lowest of slaves by choosing to wash the disciples' feet. This was an act none of the disciples were willing to stoop low enough to choose to perform because it was the responsibility of the lowest ranking member in the household to perform this task. Like us, they were constantly fighting to be in a position of authority. Is that why many today mistakenly believe they are being called to start their own ministry rather than serving in the community of Christians they are part of? Or is it why we are pleased to find someone whom we consider less than worthy ourselves? There are statistics that show that evangelicals are more likely to view beggars on the street as being unworthy because they have chosen not to work. Is this not a point of unrighteous judgement and a lack of an outpouring of love for those less fortunate? When God provided manna to the people of Israel when they were journeying to the Promised Land was there anyone excluded?

Matthew 18:1-3 King James Version (KJV)
[1] At the same time came the disciples unto Jesus, saying, Who is the greatest in the kingdom of heaven?
[2] And Jesus called a little child unto him and set him in the midst of them,
[3] And said, Verily I say unto you, Except ye be converted and become as little children, ye shall not enter into the kingdom of heaven.

Matthew 19:27-30 King James Version (KJV)
[27] Then answered Peter and said unto him, Behold, we have forsaken all and followed thee; what shall we have therefore?
[28] And Jesus said unto them, Verily I say unto you, That ye which have followed me, in the regeneration when the Son of man shall sit in the throne of his glory, ye also shall sit upon twelve thrones, judging the twelve tribes of Israel.
[29] And every one that hath forsaken houses, or brethren, or sisters, or father, or mother, or wife, or children, or lands, for my name's sake, shall receive an hundredfold and shall inherit everlasting life.
[30] But many that are first shall be last; and the last shall be first.

Mark 10:42-44 King James Version (KJV)
[42] But Jesus called them to him and saith unto them, Ye know that they which are accounted to rule over the Gentiles exercise lordship over them; and their great ones exercise authority upon them.
[43] But so shall it not be among you: but whosoever will be great among you, shall be your minister:
[44] And whosoever of you will be the chiefest, shall be servant of all.

Luke 9:46-56 King James Version (KJV)
[46] Then there arose a reasoning among them, which of them should be greatest.
[47] And Jesus, perceiving the thought of their heart, took a child and set him by him,

⁴⁸ And said unto them, Whosoever shall receive this child in my name receiveth me: and whosoever shall receive me receiveth him that sent me: for he that is least among you all, the same shall be great.

⁴⁹ And John answered and said, Master, we saw one casting out devils in thy name; and we forbad him, because he followeth not with us.

⁵⁰ And Jesus said unto him, Forbid him not: for he that is not against us is for us.

⁵¹ And it came to pass, when the time was come that he should be received up, he stedfastly set his face to go to Jerusalem,

⁵² And sent messengers before his face: and they went and entered into a village of the Samaritans, to make ready for him.

⁵³ And they did not receive him, because his face was as though he would go to Jerusalem.

⁵⁴ And when his disciples James and John saw this, they said, Lord, wilt thou that we command fire to come down from heaven and consume them, even as Elias did?

⁵⁵ But he turned and rebuked them and said, Ye know not what manner of spirit ye are of.

⁵⁶ For the Son of man is not come to destroy men's lives, but to save them. And they went to another village.

John 13:1-7 King James Version (KJV)

¹ Now before the feast of the passover, when Jesus knew that his hour was come that he should depart out of this world unto the Father, having loved his own which were in the world, he loved them unto the end.

² And supper being ended, the devil having now put into the heart of Judas Iscariot, Simon's son, to betray him;

³ Jesus knowing that the Father had given all things into his hands and that he was come from God and went to God;

⁴ He riseth from supper and laid aside his garments; and took a towel and girded himself.

⁵ After that he poureth water into a bason and began to wash the disciples' feet and to wipe them with the towel wherewith he was girded.

⁶ Then cometh he to Simon Peter: and Peter saith unto him, Lord, dost thou wash my feet?

⁷ Jesus answered and said unto him, What I do thou knowest not now; but thou shalt know hereafter.

Or maybe you are like me, while sitting under someone else's ministry I'd be thinking of how I could be doing it better than them rather than supporting them in prayer and asking the Lord to support the ministry that was being provided. Is this not the same as the disciples' refusal to stoop so low as to be the one to volunteer to wash someone else's feet? It has taken repentance, prayer and a mighty work of the Holy Spirit to make this change in me.

The conversion of my attitude started when the Holy Spirit directed me to pray to share the spirit of the minister who was delivering the message that day. All of a sudden, things changed and the power of the Spirit amplified the message being delivered so that there was no doubt God was using him. As many of you can attest to, we can feel the presence of the Holy Spirit when we allow him to be involved in our lives.

Another example I am led to have you consider is how I expressed my gratitude toward God when He saved the lives of me, my wife and my daughter. After I graduated from college, we drove by car from Rolla, Missouri to my first job as an engineer in Spokane, Washington. Twice on the way we should have been killed, but through God's intervention (His grace) we did not even get a scratch. The one instance I will share happened as we were leaving Yellowstone Park. AAA (the roadside service company) had routed us through Yellowstone Park, which is closed in January. When we halted at the entrance to Yellowstone Park, the highway patrol rerouted us to Idaho down an icy, hillside road which was barely wide enough for two lanes. This was before GPS. Well, as we were rounding a curve, with the mountain side to the left and a steep drop off of more than several hundred feet below us to a river on the left, we hit a huge rock in the middle of the highway. I could not take evasive action because there was a car coming in the opposite direction. We hit the rock and our little Volkswagen went airborne. But, instead of following the laws of motion, which dictate that the car should have went in a straight line sending us over the edge of the cliff, the car landed back on the road following the curve just as if we had never hit the rock! A short distance from this incident, we stopped in a road safe lane, which are common in this area for trucks which have brake failures. The VW had some minor damage underneath, but that was all. The driver of the other car turned and came back to see the aftermath just knowing they would find us dead. Instead, they found we had pulled off into the safe lane. They told us they were sure we had been killed. This indeed was a miracle. So, to show my gratitude, when we arrived at Spokane we found a church. I was so thankful that I reached in my pocket and took out all my loose pocket change and put it in the offering plate. Here is an example of my selfish behavior. I kept the folded bills in my wallet. It would have been more appropriate for me to testify of the miracle and open my wallet and my heart to God, but this was not what I choose to do. Here it shows how distant I was from the influences of the Holy Spirit. Yet God was still doing miracles in my life.

138

Any behavior which calls us to be set apart or above or less than the community of which we are part, can be seen as a misinterpretation of what God is calling us to be and do. The works of sin or the flesh go far beyond the Ten Commandments, which were provided to get men to know and avoid sin and to prove that through our own effort, we cannot achieve salvation.

There is a lot of fine tuning needed for us to conform to the image which God originally intended for us. He created us to be like Christ Jesus so we can be one with Him and each other. Again, if we are to be one of His followers, we need to be willing to allow the Holy Spirit to transform us by admitting that we are not performing in the way God desires. Then we need to give God the permission to purge us of our iniquity and unrighteous behaviors and implant in us God's righteous ways and along with a new heart. This can only be accomplished after we humble ourselves and admit that our prideful ways are sinful. This is an admission that we need forgiveness and admit that we are powerless to do this on our own. God can then work to transform us by the power of the Holy Spirit. Then we can be fully converted to the image and likeness of Christ Jesus of Nazareth.

CHAPTER 14

Worship In Spirit And Truth

The formula here is:

TW = M X C²

Where:

TW = True Worship

M = Man

C² = Christ Multiplied by the Comforter (the Holy Spirit)

Which translates into TW which stands for true worship equals M which stands for Man transformed by C^2 which stands for Christ multiplied through the Comforter.

John 4:24 King James Version (KJV)
[24] God is a Spirit: and they that worship him must worship him in spirit and in truth.

What is worship? Is it just cleaning up and sitting for an hour while someone preaches? Is it kneeling down in prayer? What is it? In Revelations we are shown scenes around the throne of God. In each one God is the center piece or the focal point. So, from the book of Revelations we can see that the first step in worship is to place God as our focal point or the center of our attention. Anything else is just a meeting of a group of people. Another thing we see is that those in attendance praise God for His holiness. We see reverence to God which is the recognition that He is the one who deserves honor for all things. No matter what the position or status of a given individual is, God takes preeminence. He comes first. We see a recognition that God is all powerful and deserves our allegiance. We see acts of gratitude to God. We see the righteous prayers of the saints are preserved. It also shows that only the pure in heart are allowed in the presence of God, meaning those who have been purified through the works of Jesus the Christ and His Holy Spirit.

Revelation 4:1-11 King James Version (KJV)
[1] After this I looked and, behold, a door was opened in heaven: and the first voice which I heard was as it were of a trumpet talking with me; which said, Come up hither and I will shew thee things which must be hereafter.
[2] And immediately I was in the spirit: and, behold, a throne was set in heaven and one sat on the throne.
[3] And he that sat was to look upon like a jasper and a sardine stone: and there was a rainbow round about the throne, in sight like unto an emerald.
[4] And round about the throne were four and twenty seats: and upon the seats I saw four and twenty elders sitting, clothed in white raiment; and they had on their heads crowns of gold.
[5] And out of the throne proceeded lightnings and thunderings and voices: and there were seven lamps of fire burning before the throne, which are the seven Spirits of God.
[6] And before the throne there was a sea of glass like unto crystal: and in the midst of the throne and round about the throne, were four beasts full of eyes before and behind.
[7] And the first beast was like a lion and the second beast like a calf and the third beast had a face as a man and the fourth beast was like a flying eagle.
[8] And the four beasts had each of them six wings about him; and they were full of eyes within: and they rest not day and night, saying, Holy, holy, holy, Lord God Almighty, which was and is and is to come.
[9] And when those beasts give glory and honour and thanks to him that sat on the throne, who liveth for ever and ever,
[10] The four and twenty elders fall down before him that sat on the throne and worship him that liveth for ever and ever and cast their crowns before the throne, saying,
[11] Thou art worthy, O Lord, to receive glory and honour and power: for thou hast created all things and for thy pleasure they are and were created.

In worship, we are to seek for God to open us up to repentance and open our eyes to the sin in our lives. This is so that His Holy Spirit can perform the spiritual healing which is needed in our lives, purging the sin from us so we can have God's righteousness embedded within us. We are to seek for His Holy Spirit to implant love for Him and His ways into our life. We are to seek to have spiritual gifts and the fruits of the spirit functioning among us. We are to seek guidance to perform God's will. We are to seek God's words of direction (prophecy) so that we may edify the fellowship and provide words of reproof. We are to seek God's words of correction for sin and words to those who are unbelievers, that they may come to repentance so that God can perform the spiritual healing they require. It is stated also in scripture that worship is the way we live our lives. It is something which carries through every aspect of who we are and what we do.

Proverbs 12:1-3 King James Version (KJV)

[1] Whoso loveth instruction loveth knowledge: but he that hateth reproof is brutish.

[2] A good man obtaineth favour of the Lord: but a man of wicked devices will he condemn.

[3] A man shall not be established by wickedness: but the root of the righteous shall not be moved.

2 Timothy 3:15-17 Amplified Bible (AMP)

[15] and how from childhood you have known the sacred writings (Hebrew Scriptures) which are able to give you the wisdom that leads to salvation through faith which is in Christ Jesus [surrendering your entire self to Him and having absolute confidence in His wisdom, power and goodness].

[16] All Scripture is God-breathed [given by divine inspiration] and is profitable for instruction, for conviction [of sin], for correction [of error and restoration to obedience], for training in righteousness [learning to live in conformity to God's will, both publicly and privately—behaving honorably with personal integrity and moral courage];

[17] so that the [a]man of God may be complete and proficient, outfitted and thoroughly equipped for every good work.

Footnotes:

2 Timothy 3:16 Or Every scripture inspired by God is also

Today, we are not much different in our worship than the early Israelites. They came together to worship every Sabbath but missed the true purpose for which they were gathered. We even follow a standard form of worship similar to what they did. We say a prayer, listen to scripture being read and maybe even take notes. We sing songs and baptize people. But as the following scripture states, our hearts are far from God.

Isaiah 29:13 King James Version (KJV)

[13] Wherefore the Lord said, Forasmuch as this people draw near me with their mouth and with their lips do honour me, but have removed their heart far from me and their fear[2] toward me is taught by the precept of men:

Matthew 15:9 King James Version (KJV)

[9] But in vain they do worship me, teaching for doctrines the commandments of men.

How often do we hear sermons based on human or fleshly wants and needs? Sermons on making us rich or being a better person or just words of comfort saying we are OK the way we are. Sermons about making our existence here more tolerable or comfortable. Sermons that feed the desire for us to be rich

---

[2] In some versions translated as worship

and to have the best just for ourselves or that encourage being a people who seek what we can get out of life now. Teachings based on someone's opinion or about things that have to do with worldly attitudes rather than the direction of the Holy Spirit. We hear these words often, "put in your seed offering so that you can get that hundred-fold return." Sermons to teach us how to become rich or seek self-peace through doing what makes us feel good. Or teachings that indicate world peace can come through any means other than by the work of the Holy Spirit. And many others, teachings that appeal to our lusts rather than teaching us to trust God. Teachings that focus on ways to make the ministry grow, but not on spiritual growth. Or evangelism to bring in more converts who are like us. Teachings which distort the scriptures and distort who God is and what His desires are. Teachings which say you can only use the literal interpretation of the words in scripture or that the way the minister or leaders interpret them are not guided by the Holy Spirit. Teachings that the bible needs a human to interpret and not the Holy Spirit. Many teachings are from scripture that is misconstrued or distorted to amplify man and not God. The scripture is being twisted just as Satan twisted scripture in the desert to try to trick Jesus the way he successfully tricked Eve. In short, teachings that are centered on us in this life and not focused on having this life be the same as it is in heaven; teachings not based on the guidance of the Holy Spirit, who can guide us in understanding the true meaning of the words on the pages.

We are selfish in our seeking God. It is more about what is in it for us as we desire more, More, MORE. We hear often how we were meant to be rich. We are so anxious about seeing the service be over, or I am tired and ready to go home, or ready to go out to eat, or just get out of here. We are more about us and not about God. We value our time for ourselves and not with God. It is more about duty than our love for God. I know this because I have had the same sentiments. I had not really understood that God had specific reasons for us to come to worship other than we were commanded to do so. I have been amiss in understanding that the worship service is to be about God's desires and wants and needs and not me and my wants and needs (mostly my wants). Like many of us, I attended church out of duty but there was always something more drawing me to come back. I attended church because I was taught that I needed to, but I always seemed to have something inside that kept drawing me to the preached word ever since childhood. There was something when I was a youngster in church that would cause me to remember, almost verbatim, every word being preached, but I never had a desire to study scripture. As a matter of fact, I never read the bible until I was baptized in 1975 at the age of 29.

Now don't get me wrong, I have had many wonderful experiences in worship services. Like the time in prayer service, after a very short prayer of a few of sentences, the Holy Spirit just started filling me with a feeling of warmth that started in my chest and spread throughout my entire body. I began to feel connectedness to my surroundings until I felt I was one with the very air around me and all creation. I have had many spiritual experiences such as this which continued to draw me back to church without an in-depth understanding of what God was doing. I have always seemed to understand the need for God, but did not always understand the need for the work of Jesus the Christ and the Holy Spirit. I have always had a belief in God, but kept being tempted to follow the way of the world. I have made the mistake many times of giving in to the temptation to live the worldly life. Praise be to God for the grace he has provided in Christ Jesus. Please meditate on the following scriptures.

Psalm 95:6 King James Version (KJV)
⁶ O come, let us worship and bow down: let us kneel before the Lord our maker.

Psalm 99:5 King James Version (KJV)
⁵ Exalt ye the Lord our God and worship at his footstool; for he is holy.

Psalm 100:2 King James Version (KJV)
² Serve the Lord with gladness: come before his presence with singing.

Psalm 132:7 King James Version (KJV)
⁷ We will go into his tabernacles: we will worship at his footstool.

Luke 2:37 King James Version (KJV)
³⁷ And she was a widow of about fourscore and four years, which departed not from the temple, but served God with fastings and prayers night and day.

John 4:22 King James Version (KJV)
²² Ye worship ye know not what: we know what we worship: for salvation is of the Jews.

John 9:31 King James Version (KJV)

[31] Now we know that God heareth not sinners: but if any man be a worshipper of God and doeth his will, him he heareth

Acts 13:2 King James Version (KJV)

[2] As they ministered[3] to the Lord and fasted, the Holy Ghost said, Separate me Barnabas and Saul for the work whereunto I have called them.

Romans 12:1-20 King James Version (KJV)

[1] I beseech you therefore, brethren, by the mercies of God, that ye present your bodies a living sacrifice, holy, acceptable unto God, which is your reasonable service.

[2] And be not conformed to this world: but be ye transformed by the renewing of your mind, that ye may prove what is that good and acceptable and perfect, will of God.

[3] For I say, through the grace given unto me, to every man that is among you, not to think of himself more highly than he ought to think; but to think soberly, according as God hath dealt to every man the measure of faith.

[4] For as we have many members in one body and all members have not the same office:

[5] So we, being many, are one body in Christ and every one members one of another.

[6] Having then gifts differing according to the grace that is given to us, whether prophecy, let us prophesy according to the proportion of faith;

[7] Or ministry, let us wait on our ministering: or he that teacheth, on teaching;

[8] Or he that exhorteth, on exhortation: he that giveth, let him do it with simplicity; he that ruleth, with diligence; he that sheweth mercy, with cheerfulness.

[9] Let love be without dissimulation. Abhor that which is evil; cleave to that which is good.

[10] Be kindly affectioned one to another with brotherly love; in honour preferring one another;

[11] Not slothful in business; fervent in spirit; serving the Lord;

[12] Rejoicing in hope; patient in tribulation; continuing instant in prayer;

[13] Distributing to the necessity of saints; given to hospitality.

[14] Bless them which persecute you: bless and curse not.

[15] Rejoice with them that do rejoice and weep with them that weep.

[16] Be of the same mind one toward another. Mind not high things, but condescend to men of low estate. Be not wise in your own conceits.

[17] Recompense to no man evil for evil. Provide things honest in the sight of all men.

[18] If it be possible, as much as lieth in you, live peaceably with all men.

[19] Dearly beloved, avenge not yourselves, but rather give place unto wrath: for it is written, Vengeance is mine; I will repay, saith the Lord.

[20] Therefore if thine enemy hunger, feed him; if he thirst, give him drink: for in so doing thou shalt heap coals of fire on his head.

1 Corinthians 14:14-31 King James Version (KJV)

[14] For if I pray in an unknown tongue, my spirit prayeth, but my understanding is unfruitful.

[15] What is it then? I will pray with the spirit and I will pray with the understanding also: I will sing with the spirit and I will sing with the understanding also.

---

[3] In some translations worshiped

[16] Else when thou shalt bless with the spirit, how shall he that occupieth the room of the unlearned say Amen at thy giving of thanks, seeing he understandeth not what thou sayest?

[17] For thou verily givest thanks well, but the other is not edified.

[18] I thank my God, I speak with tongues more than ye all:

[19] Yet in the church I had rather speak five words with my understanding, that by my voice I might teach others also, than ten thousand words in an unknown tongue.

[20] Brethren, be not children in understanding: howbeit in malice be ye children, but in understanding be men.

[21] In the law it is written, With men of other tongues and other lips will I speak unto this people; and yet for all that will they not hear me, saith the Lord.

[22] Wherefore tongues are for a sign, not to them that believe, but to them that believe not: but prophesying serveth not for them that believe not, but for them which believe.

[23] If therefore the whole church be come together into one place and all speak with tongues and there come in those that are unlearned, or unbelievers, will they not say that ye are mad?

[24] But if all prophesy and there come in one that believeth not, or one unlearned, he is convinced of all, he is judged of all:

[25] And thus are the secrets of his heart made manifest; and so falling down on his face he will worship God and report that God is in you of a truth.

[26] How is it then, brethren? when ye come together, every one of you hath a psalm, hath a doctrine, hath a tongue, hath a revelation, hath an interpretation. Let all things be done unto edifying.

[27] If any man speak in an unknown tongue, let it be by two, or at the most by three and that by course; and let one interpret.

[28] But if there be no interpreter, let him keep silence in the church; and let him speak to himself and to God.

[29] Let the prophets speak two or three and let the other judge.

[30] If any thing be revealed to another that sitteth by, let the first hold his peace.

[31] For ye may all prophesy one by one, that all may learn and all may be comforted.

For us to truly worship requires preparation, willingness and a knowledge of what worship is about. It is time for us to quit walking in fleshly lusts and iniquity. We need to start walking in God's righteousness by the power of the Holy Spirit to allow the Holy Spirit to fulfill the purpose for which He was given.

Preparation for worship is an everyday endeavor. We must be willing to follow the direction of the Holy Spirit to do things God's way. We are to follow His righteousness and honor Him in all that we do. Then we must pray for direction for things we can do to add to the worship of Him. When we enter into worship, we should come in with clean bodies and clothing, as well as a clean spirit. We should be prepared to allow Him to cleanse our spirit of all unrighteousness. We should come to worship Him and be joyful that we can enter in His presence. We should not want to contaminate the worship experience in any way. We should be prepared to follow the leader of the service so that all things will be done in order. The leader should be prepared to follow the lead of the Lord for guidance on who should offer the various gifts that he has provided for them to share. As in all things pray... pray... pray.

1 Thessalonians 5:16-18 King James Version (KJV)
[16] Rejoice evermore.
[17] Pray without ceasing.
[18] In every thing give thanks: for this is the will of God in Christ Jesus concerning you.

We have become so insensitive to His guidance that we have to have a printed program to ensure an orderly service. This is okay for a meeting. But for true worship, the order needs to be directed by God so we have to be led by Him in what we do. If that is by a printed order then let it be, so as long as it is set by guidance of the Holy Spirit.

I know for years as a pastor, I would just copy the service order from the previous week, try to figure out who was available to speak and ask if they were willing to do so. Many times, the Holy Spirit would point me to someone, but they would refuse to provide the ministry that God wanted to perform through them. Sometimes the speaker would forget (as I do sometimes) that they were the speaker of the hour. Even when I forget, I always try to be open to the guidance of the Holy Spirit to carry His message to the people. I now come prepared to have God use me, if that is His will, whether I am scheduled in the printed order of service or not.

I am led to share this experience. There was one occasion when I had gone to my home town for a family reunion. The culmination of this was an invitation for any family member that wished to attend the home congregation of one of elders in the family. During the service, I was introduced as a minister to the congregation. Then the pastor called me up front and asked if I would provide the message for the day! I was a little taken back because most Baptist ministers do not offer the pulpit to non-Baptist ministers. Through the direction and power of the Holy Spirit, I was able to deliver a sermon which ministered to those in attendance. By the way, the service was celebrating young members who were graduates. I was led to provide a sermon which was pointed to them and how we as members of the body should support them. God is so good. He uses us when we are willing. The power of His spirit is ever resident in us to perform the work of God when we are open to him. I was able to do this only because I know when I get up to speak, it is the Spirit which provides the words that His people need and I always pray for this to happen. I have also been an ardent student of the scripture so the Holy Spirit is able to call to my remembrance the essence of the scripture for each sermon I deliver.

True worship is something that has to be orchestrated by the Holy Spirit and not by what we think. It is something that is not a fleshly, man thing, but a spiritual endeavor. I know God does not need me to use my intelligence to perform His ministry. He showed me this one day in a service when he used my tongue to deliver words of prophecy to His people. I had no control over what he did. I was standing singing a praise song. The only involvement I had was that he used my voice box to speak words of love and compassion to His people. These words came forth that day. I have never forgotten them.

"It is my desire for my people to enter into my presence so that they may be healed."

This act was witnessed by several people standing around me. This was the first occasion which God provided a word of prophesy through me. I was taken back and did not understand what had happened, but one of the other ministers took me aside and told me what had just occurred.

I now know when God wants me to prophesy because I have experienced His nudging. It is so powerful at times that I feel as though I will explode if I do not say what I am being led to say. But, in order for the service to remain orderly, I always get the leader's permission first before I deliver the message God wants me to deliver.

In conclusion, be prepared to offer the gifts of the spirit which God has provided specifically for you. Live a life of preparation. Humble yourself and allow God to rejuvenate you so that you will not disrupt the flow of the Holy Spirit. Without being led by the Holy Spirit we worship in vain.

John 4:24 King James Version (KJV)

24 God is a Spirit: and they that worship him must worship him in spirit and in truth.

John 3:5-7 King James Version (KJV)

5 Jesus answered, Verily, verily, I say unto thee, Except a man be born of water and of the Spirit, he cannot enter into the kingdom of God.

6 That which is born of the flesh is flesh; and that which is born of the Spirit is spirit.

7 Marvel not that I said unto thee, Ye must be born again.

CHAPTER 15

Pray For Workers

Matthew 9:37-38 King James Version (KJV)
[37] Then saith he unto his disciples, The harvest truly is plenteous, but the labourers are few;
[38] Pray ye therefore the Lord of the harvest, that he will send forth labourers into his harvest.

1 Corinthians 3:9 King James Version (KJV)
[9] For we are labourers together with God: ye are God's husbandry, ye are God's building.

1 Corinthians 3:5-17 Amplified Bible (AMP)
[5] What then is Apollos? And what is Paul? Just servants through whom you believed [in Christ], even as the Lord appointed to each his task.
[6] I planted, Apollos watered, but God [all the while] was causing the growth.
[7] So neither is the one who plants nor the one who waters anything, but [only] God who causes the growth.
[8] He who plants and he who waters are one [in importance and esteem, working toward the same purpose]; but each will receive his own reward according to his own labor.
[9] For we are God's fellow workers [His servants working together]; you are God's cultivated field [His garden, His vineyard], God's building.
[10] According to the [remarkable] grace of God which was given to me [to prepare me for my task], like a skillful master builder I laid a foundation and now another is building on it. But each one must be careful how he builds on it,
[11] for no one can lay a foundation other than the one which is [already] laid, which is Jesus Christ.
[12] But if anyone builds on the foundation with gold, silver, precious stones, wood, hay, straw,
[13] each one's work will be clearly shown [for what it is]; for the day [of judgment] will disclose it, because it is to be revealed with fire and the fire will test the quality and character and worth of each person's work.
[14] If any person's work which he has built [on this foundation, that is, any outcome of his effort] remains [and survives this test], he will receive a reward.

¹⁵ But if any person's work is burned up [by the test], he will suffer the loss [of his reward]; yet he himself will be saved, but only as [one who has barely escaped] through fire.

¹⁶ Do you not know and understand that you [the church] are the temple of God and that the Spirit of God dwells [permanently] in you [collectively and individually]?

¹⁷ If anyone destroys the temple of God [corrupting it with false doctrine], God will destroy the destroyer; for the temple of God is holy (sacred) and that is what you are.

The formula here is:

GW = M X C²

Where:

GW = Workers in God's Kingdom

M = Man

C² = Christ with the Comforter (the Holy Spirit)

As I have stated previously, there are three spirits working in this world. One is the spirit of Man (many times referred to as the flesh in scripture). Another is the spirit of the devil or Satan or the evil one. The third is the Holy Spirit. Each of these has one intent and one purpose. The flesh or the spirit of man uncorrected by the Holy Spirit seeks selfish gains. The spirit of the devil uses any means necessary to keep us from following the spirit of God which leads us to revere and serve God and to receive the salvation that is provided in Christ Jesus. In scripture, Satan is called the father of lies because all he will tell is lies as this is his true nature.

John 8:44 King James Version (KJV)
⁴⁴ Ye are of your father the devil and the lusts of your father ye will do. He was a murderer from the beginning and abode not in the truth, because there is no truth in him. When he speaketh a lie, he speaketh of his own: for he is a liar and the father of it.

One of the tasks of the Holy Spirit is to provide spiritual energy to perform the tasks which God has specifically stated we should perform. These tasks are not always fully evident to us but if we follow the direction of the Holy Spirit he will provide the direction and power needed for us to complete the work God has given us. Take the example of Abraham (or Abram at the time God called him to leave his home). God told him to take up his family and leave the place he was and move to another location. He did not reveal this location to him until he got there. God does not always reveal where we are to go or what we are to do but always be obedient and His blessings will follow.

Genesis 12:1-4 King James Version (KJV)
[1] Now the Lord had said unto Abram, Get thee out of thy country and from thy kindred and from thy father's house, unto a land that I will shew thee:
[2] And I will make of thee a great nation and I will bless thee and make thy name great; and thou shalt be a blessing:
[3] And I will bless them that bless thee and curse him that curseth thee: and in thee shall all families of the earth be blessed.
[4] So Abram departed, as the Lord had spoken unto him; and Lot went with him: and Abram was seventy and five years old when he departed out of Haran.

The work we are called to varies by individual. The work of an Apostle is to be a witness for Christ Jesus of His reality and His salvation. Then there are those such as Dorcas and Stephen in scripture who were appointed to perform tasks ordained for them to perform. Dorcas saw to the needs of the poor by making gifts of clothing. Stephen saw to the needs of the church by serving meals and the gospel to believers. Some of the other tasks we are called to perform are listed as gifts of the Spirit in scripture. God provides the ability for each of us to perform the tasks provided based on our obedience to him. We may not even be aware that we have a special calling but it can become very evident when we sit back and review the things we consistently do in God's name. In my case I can identify that among others was the ministry that I performed to youth in the church. I just took it for granted it was a work which needed to be done so I did it. I was not always willing but something kept me doing those things. also. Now I know it was God ordained and I was following the direction of The Holy Spirit.

I know many try to force the issue and seek to know upfront what our spiritual gifts are. In most cases, we won't get that data until God in His wisdom sees it necessary to provide this information to us. We usually just stumble onto the gift as we are led by the Holy Spirit to perform repetitive tasks. Most of the time others will see the gifts working in us long before we see them as such. What we need to do to discover these, is to prayerfully follow the lead of the Holy Spirit. He will guide us in the right direction. Then there are others which have obvious gifts such as those who are prophets. There are many such identified in the scripture, both men and women.

Section 46 Doctrine & Covenants 46:6b-8b
[Sec 46:6b] And again, it is given by the Holy Ghost to some to know the diversities of

153

operations, whether it be of God, that the manifestations of the Spirit may be given to every man to profit withal.

[Sec 46:7a] And again, verily I say unto you, To some it is given, by the Spirit of God, the word of wisdom;

[Sec 46:7b] to another it is given the word of knowledge, that all may be taught to be wise and to have knowledge.

[Sec 46:7c] And again, to some it is given to have faith to be healed and to others it is given to have faith to heal.

[Sec 46:7d] And again, to some it is given the workings of miracles; and to others it is given to prophesy and to others the discerning of spirits.

[Sec 46:7e] And again, it is given to some to speak with tongues and to another it is given the interpretation of tongues:

[Sec 46:7f] and all these gifts come from God, for the benefit of the children of God.

[Sec 46:7g] And unto the bishop of the church and unto such as God shall appoint and ordain to watch over the church and to be elders unto the church, are to have it given unto them to discern all those gifts, lest there be any among you professing and yet be not of God.

[Sec 46:8a] And it shall come to pass that he that asketh in spirit shall receive in spirit; that unto some it may be given to have all those gifts, that there may be a head, in order that every member may be profited thereby:

[Sec 46:8b] he that asketh in the spirit, asketh according to the will of God, wherefore it is done

The key to the work we are called is obedience to the Holy Spirit and learning to discern His guidance. This comes along with our spiritual conditioning and maturity through prayer and fasting. Remember God will not force us to do anything we don't want to. So, it takes a conversion experience to cause us to become aware of God's purposes for us and for us to be true workers in His kingdom. Take for instance Paul and his road to Damascus experience or when he was led to go to Rome at the end of his ministry. He only knew what he was to do when the Holy Spirit directed him. He didn't always understand or even recognize each of the gifts of the spirit he had but he just did as directed by the Holy Spirit at each point in time. He knew after fasting and prayer that his calling was to take the witness of Christ Jesus to the Gentiles. He knew that in doing this, the Holy Spirit would work through him to perform miracles for those who were willing to accept the work of Christ in their lives, or when God chose for him to be used by the Holy Spirit to perform miracles to edify the church. Workers are needed to edify the church through the calling God places upon us. Some of the more prominent gifts will become very evident. Others we may not understand or know about for years. As scripture states, God works in mysterious ways His miracles to perform. As we become closer to God, we will become more aware of how He is using us to do the work He has ordained for us. We are a doorway for the Spirit to perform the mysterious conversion that true believers can receive when they are willing to build God's Kingdom on earth. This is why we need to perform the work to take the message as far as we can as Jesus taught in the Lord's Prayer:

Luke 11:2 King James Version (KJV)
[2] And he said unto them, When ye pray, say, Our Father which art in heaven, Hallowed be thy name. Thy kingdom come. Thy will be done, as in heaven, so in earth.

We who are written in the Lamb's book of life need to be made aware that this kingdom can only come when all of us fulfill our part. As scripture states none of us can be made perfect until all are come unto the service of Him.

2 Timothy 3:17 King James Version (KJV)
[17] That the man of God may be perfect, thoroughly furnished unto all good works.

2 Kings 23:24 King James Version (KJV)
[24] Moreover the workers with familiar spirits and the wizards and the images and the idols and all the abominations that were spied in the land of Judah and in Jerusalem, did Josiah put away, that he might perform the words of the law which were written in the book that Hilkiah the priest found in the house of the Lord.

Psalm 5:5 King James Version (KJV)
[5] The foolish shall not stand in thy sight: thou hatest all workers of iniquity.

Proverbs 10:29 King James Version (KJV)
[29] The way of the Lord is strength to the upright: but destruction shall be to the workers of iniquity.

Luke 13:27King James Version (KJV)
[27] But he shall say, I tell you, I know you not whence ye are; depart from me, all ye workers of iniquity.

1 Corinthians 12:1-14 King James Version (KJV)
[1] Now concerning spiritual gifts, brethren, I would not have you ignorant.
[2] Ye know that ye were Gentiles, carried away unto these dumb idols, even as ye were led.
[3] Wherefore I give you to understand, that no man speaking by the Spirit of God calleth Jesus accursed: and that no man can say that Jesus is the Lord, but by the Holy Ghost.
[4] Now there are diversities of gifts, but the same Spirit.
[5] And there are differences of administrations, but the same Lord.
[6] And there are diversities of operations, but it is the same God which worketh all in all.
[7] But the manifestation of the Spirit is given to every man to profit withal.
[8] For to one is given by the Spirit the word of wisdom; to another the word of knowledge by the same Spirit;

155

⁹ To another faith by the same Spirit; to another the gifts of healing by the same Spirit;

¹⁰ To another the working of miracles; to another prophecy; to another discerning of spirits; to another divers kinds of tongues; to another the interpretation of tongues:

¹¹ But all these worketh that one and the selfsame Spirit, dividing to every man severally as he will.

¹² For as the body is one and hath many members and all the members of that one body, being many, are one body: so also is Christ.

¹³ For by one Spirit are we all baptized into one body, whether we be Jews or Gentiles, whether we be bond or free; and have been all made to drink into one Spirit.

¹⁴ For the body is not one member, but many.

1 Corinthians 13:1-13 King James Version (KJV)

¹ Though I speak with the tongues of men and of angels and have not charity, I am become as sounding brass, or a tinkling cymbal.

² And though I have the gift of prophecy and understand all mysteries and all knowledge; and though I have all faith, so that I could remove mountains and have not charity, I am nothing.

³ And though I bestow all my goods to feed the poor and though I give my body to be burned and have not charity, it profiteth me nothing.

⁴ Charity suffereth long and is kind; charity envieth not; charity vaunteth not itself, is not puffed up,

⁵ Doth not behave itself unseemly, seeketh not her own, is not easily provoked, thinketh no evil;

⁶ Rejoiceth not in iniquity, but rejoiceth in the truth;

⁷ Beareth all things, believeth all things, hopeth all things, endureth all things.

⁸ Charity never faileth: but whether there be prophecies, they shall fail; whether there be tongues, they shall cease; whether there be knowledge, it shall vanish away.

⁹ For we know in part and we prophesy in part.

¹⁰ But when that which is perfect is come, then that which is in part shall be done away.

¹¹ When I was a child, I spake as a child, I understood as a child, I thought as a child: but when I became a man, I put away childish things.

¹² For now we see through a glass, darkly; but then face to face: now I know in part; but then shall I know even as also I am known.

¹³ And now abideth faith, hope, charity, these three; but the greatest of these is charity.

2 Corinthians 6:1-3 King James Version (KJV)

¹ We then, as workers together with him, beseech you also that ye receive not the grace of God in vain.

² (For he saith, I have heard thee in a time accepted and in the day of salvation have I succoured thee: behold, now is the accepted time; behold, now is the day of salvation.)

³ Giving no offence in any thing, that the ministry be not blamed:

2 Corinthians 11:7-14 King James Version (KJV)

⁷ Have I committed an offence in abasing myself that ye might be exalted, because I have preached to you the gospel of God freely?

⁸ I robbed other churches, taking wages of them, to do you service.

9 And when I was present with you and wanted, I was chargeable to no man: for that which was lacking to me the brethren which came from Macedonia supplied: and in all things I have kept myself from being burdensome unto you and so will I keep myself.

10 As the truth of Christ is in me, no man shall stop me of this boasting in the regions of Achaia.

11 Wherefore? because I love you not? God knoweth.

12 But what I do, that I will do, that I may cut off occasion from them which desire occasion; that wherein they glory, they may be found even as we.

13 For such are false apostles, deceitful workers, transforming themselves into the apostles of Christ.

14 And no marvel; for Satan himself is transformed into an angel of light.

2 Corinthians 11:7-14 Amplified Bible (AMP)

7 Or did I [perhaps] sin by humbling myself so that you might be exalted and honored, because I preached God's gospel to you [c]free of charge?

8 I robbed other churches by accepting [more than their share of] financial support for my ministry to you.

9 And when I was with you and ran short [financially], I did not burden any of you; for what I needed was fully supplied by the brothers (Silas and Timothy) who came from Macedonia (the church at Philippi). So I kept myself from being a burden to you in any way and will continue to do so.

10 As the truth of Christ is in me, my boast [of independence] will not be silenced in the regions of Achaia (southern Greece).

11 Why? Because I do not love you [or wish you well, or have regard for your welfare]? God knows [that I do]!

12 But what I am doing I will keep doing, [for I am determined to keep this independence] in order to cut off the claim of those who want an opportunity to be regarded just as we are in the things they brag about.

13 For such men are counterfeit apostles, deceitful workers, masquerading as apostles of Christ.

14 And no wonder, since Satan himself masquerades as an angel of light.

2 Corinthians 6:1-3 King James Version (KJV)

1 We then, as workers together with him, beseech you also that ye receive not the grace of God in vain.

2 (For he saith, I have heard thee in a time accepted, and in the day of salvation have I succoured thee: behold, now is the accepted time; behold, now is the day of salvation.)

3 Giving no offence in any thing, that the ministry be not blamed:

Philippians 3:1-3 King James Version (KJV)

1 Finally, my brethren, rejoice in the Lord. To write the same things to you, to me indeed is not grievous, but for you it is safe.

2 Beware of dogs, beware of evil workers, beware of the concision.

3 For we are the circumcision, which worship God in the spirit and rejoice in Christ Jesus and have no confidence in the flesh.

Philippians 3:1-3 Amplified Bible, Classic Edition (AMPC)

[1] For the rest, my brethren, delight yourselves in the Lord and continue to rejoice that you are in Him. To keep writing to you [over and over] of the same things is not irksome to me and it is [a precaution] for your safety.

[2] Look out for those dogs [Judaizers, legalists], look out for those mischief-makers, look out for those who mutilate the flesh.

[3] For we [Christians] are the true circumcision, who worship God in spirit and by the Spirit of God and exult and glory and pride ourselves in Jesus Christ and put no confidence or dependence [on what we are] in the flesh and on outward privileges and physical advantages and external appearances—

Isaiah 6:8 King James Version (KJV)

[8] Also I heard the voice of the Lord, saying, Whom shall I send and who will go for us? Then said I, Here am I; send me.

Matthew 9:37-38 King James Version (KJV)

[37] Then saith he unto his disciples, The harvest truly is plenteous, but the labourers are few;

[38] Pray ye therefore the Lord of the harvest, that he will send forth labourers into his harvest.

even as he asketh.

Section 46 Doctrine and Covenants 46:9a-9b

[Sec 46:9a] And again I say unto you, All things must be done in the name of Christ, whatsoever

you do in the spirit;

[Sec 46:9b] and ye must give thanks unto God in the spirit for whatever blessing ye are blessed with; and ye must practice virtue and holiness before me continually. Even so. Amen.

Have you heard of the phrase "burnout?" This is a condition which happens when someone is working in his or her own strength to do what they feel they should do, instead of listening to the Holy Spirit and allowing him to lead them in the part of the work of God suited for them. Like the apostle Paul, those truly empowered by the Holy Spirit do not run out gas. Our bodies grow tired, but all power is available in the Holy Spirit which is the same spirit that aided in the creation. This same spirit is in us when we are converted. When we work by the power of the Holy Spirit, our bodies may get tired, but we will not "burnout." When we are using the power of the Holy Spirit, the desire and ability to do God's work is endless. The ministry of the apostles demonstrates this in scripture.

So why do we need to pray for more workers? The reason is that until we as a people are ready to respond to God's calling we cannot be used by him. For example, I had to make a choice to accept the path to move up in management at my job and allow them to control what I could do, or to accept my role and use my talents as an engineer to make a living. Now, it doesn't mean that being in upper management is wrong. But it was wrong for me. Because of some of my traits, that management position would have pulled me further from God rather than closer to Him. Others may not have these tendencies in their character. I do. So, I made a conscious choice to not pursue upper management because it would have been a disaster for me, my family and most of all, my relationship with God. God helped me to see this. It would have left me with less time to work with youth and my ministry in the church and eventually could have led to me having to abandon my family. These were things God would not have preferred. Now I understand that I did not pursue this track in life because for me, success was not in titles, but in following God's lead in my life.

Many choose to place living a life of ease, pleasure, comfort and self-aggrandizement (hedonism) ahead of the life God ordained. They have no image of the eternal, only the present state of life. That does not mean they have lost their salvation, it just means they have hindered the building of God's Kingdom on earth. We all lose out because the part they should be playing is lacking. Others try to take up the slack, but because this is not their gift, it leaves holes in the work of the kingdom building. It's like putting together a puzzle that has pieces missing. No matter what you do with a puzzle like that, it will always be incomplete. Doing the work of God will not always lead to a life of ease (earthly pleasure) until we all do our part in following the Holy Spirit in the tasks we are ordained to perform. When we all respond to the call of being God's workers then we will have true peace and joy and there will be no poor or needy among us

Luke 1:16-17 King James Version (KJV)
[16] And many of the children of Israel shall he turn to the Lord their God.
[17] And he shall go before him in the spirit and power of Elias, to turn the hearts of the fathers to the children and the disobedient to the wisdom of the just; to make ready a people prepared for the Lord.

Acts 1:10-11 King James Version (KJV)
[10] And while they looked stedfastly toward heaven as he went up, behold, two men stood by them in white apparel;
[11] Which also said, Ye men of Galilee, why stand ye gazing up into heaven? this same Jesus, which is taken up from you into heaven, shall so come in like manner as ye have seen him go into heaven.

1 John 3:2 King James Version (KJV)

[2] Beloved, now are we the sons of God and it doth not yet appear what we shall be: but we know that, when he shall appear, we shall be like him; for we shall see him as he is.

CHAPTER 16

Ask And It Will Be Given To You

The formula here is

RP = M X C²

Where:

RP = Righteous Praying

M = Man

C² = Christ X Comforter (the Holy Spirit)

When we pray the mandate is that we pray righteously. This encompasses a lot. The disciples asked Jesus how to pray. This goes to show it is not a natural thing to do even for those who are religious minded. So Jesus told the disciples to pray in this manner.

Matthew 6:9-13 King James Version (KJV)
[9] After this manner therefore pray ye: Our Father which art in heaven, Hallowed be thy name.
[10] Thy kingdom come, Thy will be done in earth, as it is in heaven.
[11] Give us this day our daily bread.
[12] And forgive us our debts, as we forgive our debtors.
[13] And lead us not into temptation, but deliver us from evil: For thine is the kingdom and the power and the glory, for ever. Amen.

Also in Luke

Luke 11:1-4 King James Version (KJV)
[1] And it came to pass, that, as he was praying in a certain place, when he ceased, one of his disciples said unto him, Lord, teach us to pray, as John also taught his disciples.
[2] And he said unto them, When ye pray, say, Our Father which art in heaven, Hallowed be thy name. Thy kingdom come. Thy will be done, as in heaven, so in earth.
[3] Give us day by day our daily bread.

⁴ And forgive us our sins; for we also forgive every one that is indebted to us. And lead us not into temptation; but deliver us from evil.

Note in both of these recitations Christ was teaching not only words but the method prayer should follow and what is right to pray for in the eyes of God. As it states in scripture all things have a set of laws or rules which they must follow (that God established from the creation of the universe). In this case Jesus was imparting the rules which surround prayer. These are:

- We must pray to the only true and living God.
- We must pray in reverence to the God of all creation and recognize His authority.
- What we pray for must be in line with the Father's will.
- We must recognize the need for repentance in our lives.
- We must recognize that we forgive others and trust God to punish justly.
- Jesus points out that we should forgive like He does otherwise the forgiveness which he has provided is not truly accepted because His love is not in us.
- We must recognize we need God's help in fighting temptation. God does not cause us to be tempted to do evil. However, if that is what we choose He will allow us to follow our desires.
- God is aware of your needs and will see to those which are vital.
- We need God's protection from the evil one and ourselves because we are easily drawn into temptation.
- Note the majority of this prayer is devoted to the work which God performs for us and wants us to accept.

There are many books on prayer so this short-inspired dissertation is not to be something which surpasses them but a way to point to the keys that govern true prayer. The other rules which are not so obvious are scattered throughout scripture. Proper prayer needs the guidance and help of the Holy Spirit because as scripture states the Holy Spirit intercedes for us because we don't know what to pray for. Our understanding of God's ways is limited as we do not have a broad enough overview of what we need to do to be in agreement with Him. This can only be provided through the power of the Holy Spirit. We need to come to a knowledge of God's purposes and His plan for man. Many times, we pray based on our understanding or what we consider is needed, but it's not what God wants.

Romans 8:25-27 King James Version (KJV)
[25] But if we hope for that we see not, then do we with patience wait for it.
[26] Likewise the Spirit also helpeth our infirmities: for we know not what we should pray for as we ought: but the Spirit itself maketh intercession for us with groanings which cannot be uttered.
[27] And he that searcheth the hearts knoweth what is the mind of the Spirit, because he maketh intercession for the saints according to the will of God.

For an example of being misdirected in what we need, consider how in the following scripture the people asked Moses to pray to get rid of the serpents. But Moses was directed by God to pray for a symbol for healing of the people. This was because God wanted the people to direct their attention Him and to trust Him to heal them and be their protection, not for them to be removed from the danger of the snakes. Is that not in line with our desires today? We want to have evil removed and not trust God to be our protector. This is an example that God's purpose did not align with the requests of His followers. Their understanding of God and His purposes were far from those of God's. So, God had Moses address Him based on that which was in agreement with His purposed plan for His followers. They did not ask for something wrong, but what they asked for was not in accordance with the plan of God. They were being directed by human fear, not their trust in God. Their vision of God was limited and clouded by their situation. In the following scripture, God specifically demonstrates that many times we ask based on our wants, which do not always agree with those of God:

Numbers 21:6-8 King James Version (KJV)
[6] And the LORD sent fiery serpents among the people and they bit the people; and much people of Israel died.
[7] Therefore the people came to Moses and said, We have sinned, for we have spoken against the LORD and against thee; pray unto the LORD, that he take away the serpents from us. And Moses prayed for the people.
[8] And the LORD said unto Moses, Make thee a fiery serpent and set it upon a pole: and it shall come to pass, that every one that is bitten, when he looketh upon it, shall live.

God will not go against the free will of man. If we want to live in sin He will allow us to do so that we may learn from our actions. Therefore, we can choose to either follow our conscience of what is right or go against it and choose wrong. Hence choosing our own judgement.

Hebrews 4:11-13 King James Version (KJV)
[11] Let us labour therefore to enter into that rest, lest any man fall after the same example of unbelief.
[12] For the word of God is quick and powerful and sharper than any two edged sword, piercing even to the dividing asunder of soul and spirit and of the joints and marrow and is a discerner of the thoughts and intents of the heart.
[13] Neither is there any creature that is not manifest in his sight: but all things are naked and opened unto the eyes of him with whom we have to do.

God will not allow the children of God to be cursed. His will is for them to receive His blessing. It is only when we sin and are disobedient that He will allow us to receive the results of our sin and withdraw His protection. An example is when the King asked Balaam to curse the people of Israel. Balaam knew that God would not allow him to curse the people of God, but Balaam also knew that when God's people sinned, God would have to withdraw His protection and allow them to receive the results for their disobedience if they did not repent.

- God will not answer prayer if it is something that is of a selfish nature or that only gratifies us, or causes injury to others, or goes against His will.
- He will not recognize prayer which is not truthful or is just for the sake of show and pretense. When we approach him it has to be genuine.
- Just because we think that what we are asking in prayer is right, it doesn't mean that God sees what we are asking for as best for us. He will always defer to the greater good.
- God enjoys us discussing with him all our concerns.
- He desires for us to follow righteousness. God will only support us in those things which are righteous.
- He will not answer prayer that will cause us to move away from him or which he knows we can do using the talents which he has provided. He will not cripple us, nor will he do things to weaken us.
- He will not answer a prayer which will cause us to depend on something other than Him and the Holy Spirit.

164

- He will not provide an answer which goes against His righteousness. Someone might pray for Him to OK sexual sin because they think it's permissible if they "love" someone, even if it's outside of marriage (fornication). He will not provide an OK to unrighteous behavior of any sort. We have His commandments in scripture which most won't even read or understand when they do read them.

His approval is not indicated just because we have a good feeling about what we want. This must be done through the Holy Spirit. Yes, He will cause a feeling to come when we are agreement with Him, but this is not about feeling happy with our decisions. There are many who continue in sin because they feel good about it. Feeling good and the conformation of the Holy Spirit are two different things.

His will for us is for us to learn to choose the same things He does. So He will allow us to make our own choices; to see His ways work and to draw us more to Him. He does not want us to be robots programed to only follow a straight set of instructions but He does provide instructions on how to determine what is right and the ability to choose right through the power of the Holy Spirit. That is why the law by itself cannot save anyone.

Daniel 9:16-18 King James Version (KJV)

[16] O LORD, according to all thy righteousness, I beseech thee, let thine anger and thy fury be turned away from thy city Jerusalem, thy holy mountain: because for our sins and for the iniquities of our fathers, Jerusalem and thy people are become a reproach to all that are about us.

[17] Now therefore, O our God, hear the prayer of thy servant and his supplications and cause thy face to shine upon thy sanctuary that is desolate, for the Lord's sake.

[18] O my God, incline thine ear and hear; open thine eyes and behold our desolations and the city which is called by thy name: for we do not present our supplications before thee for our righteousnesses, but for thy great mercies.

CHAPTER 17

How Sin Is Conceived (Overcoming Temptation)

James 1:12-24 King James Version (KJV)
[12] Blessed is the man that endureth temptation: for when he is tried, he shall receive the crown of life, which the Lord hath promised to them that love him.
[13] Let no man say when he is tempted, I am tempted of God: for God cannot be tempted with evil, neither tempteth he any man:
[14] But every man is tempted, when he is drawn away of his own lust and enticed.
[15] Then when lust hath conceived, it bringeth forth sin: and sin, when it is finished, bringeth forth death.
[16] Do not err, my beloved brethren.
[17] Every good gift and every perfect gift is from above and cometh down from the Father of lights, with whom is no variableness, neither shadow of turning.
[18] Of his own will begat he us with the word of truth, that we should be a kind of firstfruits of his creatures.
[19] Wherefore, my beloved brethren, let every man be swift to hear, slow to speak, slow to wrath:
[20] For the wrath of man worketh not the righteousness of God.
[21] Wherefore lay apart all filthiness and superfluity of naughtiness and receive with meekness the engrafted word, which is able to save your souls.
[22] But be ye doers of the word and not hearers only, deceiving your own selves.
[23] For if any be a hearer of the word and not a doer, he is like unto a man beholding his natural face in a glass:
[24] For he beholdeth himself and goeth his way and straightway forgetteth what manner of man he was.

The equation here is

$$OT = M \times C^2$$

Where:

OT = Overcoming Temptation

M = man

C^2 = Christ X the Comforter (the Holy Spirit)

God demonstrated in the life of Jesus the Christ just as he was tempted of the devil we will also face temptation. When Jesus ended His forty days fast and Satan felt he would be at His weakest. Satan appeared to him offering a set of temptations. But Jesus was able to withstand them all. Scripture states that Jesus was tempted in every way that man can be tempted.

Matthew 4:1-10 King James Version (KJV)
[1] Then was Jesus led up of the Spirit into the wilderness to be tempted of the devil.
[2] And when he had fasted forty days and forty nights, he was afterward an hungred.
[3] And when the tempter came to him, he said, If thou be the Son of God, command that these stones be made bread.
[4] But he answered and said, It is written, Man shall not live by bread alone, but by every word that proceedeth out of the mouth of God.
[5] Then the devil taketh him up into the holy city and setteth him on a pinnacle of the temple,
[6] And saith unto him, If thou be the Son of God, cast thyself down: for it is written, He shall give his angels charge concerning thee: and in their hands they shall bear thee up, lest at any time thou dash thy foot against a stone.
[7] Jesus said unto him, It is written again, Thou shalt not tempt the Lord thy God.
[8] Again, the devil taketh him up into an exceeding high mountain and sheweth him all the kingdoms of the world and the glory of them;
[9] And saith unto him, All these things will I give thee, if thou wilt fall down and worship me.
[10] Then saith Jesus unto him, Get thee hence, Satan: for it is written, Thou shalt worship the Lord thy God and him only shalt thou serve.

These temptations were to:

1. Turn rocks into bread to suit his own personal needs and distrust God to provide for him. God provides scripture for reproof and instruction not as a tool for sorcery. He also provides it so that it will lead to Him and not away from Him. Jesus also understood following what seems right is not always God's righteousness. Jesus understood God and His purposes and would not try to circumvent them.

2. Then, on a high pinnacle of the temple where Satan knew he could garner the awe of all, Satan told Jesus to call upon the angels of God to keep himself from injury or death. Jesus knows God, so He understood that there was no need for Him to challenge whether God was real and ever present. Jesus had already met with the angels of God and he knew their mission. He knew of God's existence and had experienced His presence, so he understood God.

3. The ultimate temptation was to have unlimited power through the worship of someone else other than God (self-aggrandizement). Jesus again knew all power is in the hands of God and is God ordained. He knew that no one else can give this power to anyone and that above all else, we should worship and serve God the Father and no other being.

In each of these, Satan challenges whether Jesus is the Son of God or not, which is a way of denying that God sent Jesus and denying if Jesus' claims were true.

First, we must understand that we can resist temptation just as Jesus did. We must also understand that our weaknesses are very obvious to those in the spirit realm and in most cases, to the world around us. This is the point of attack in our temptations. The scripture above points to the fact that temptation is born of our own lusts, or things that are already part of our makeup.

Second, we must understand what steps are involved in temptation. Then we must understand how to fight temptation. For us to be able to withstand temptation, we must follow the works of the Holy Spirit or God's righteousness in our lives. If we live by His righteousness empowered through the Holy Spirit, we can avoid temptation altogether. But since we have not yet reached this perfect state, we have to realize that we have ruling within us sinful lusts which are the works of the flesh. Simply put, the works of the flesh (our self-centered desires and lust) lead us to consider ourselves above the common good or God's design for what is best for us all. Do no harm to anyone. If we cause injury to anyone, we all suffer.

As the above scripture states, sin starts as lust (our own selfish desires) which only considers us and no one else. Lust can be expressed in many different ways. This can be for our own pleasure, self-aggrandizement, greed or just wanting to have our way without consideration of the harm it can cause. Just consider the Ten Commandments. They give us insight into some of the ways lust can be expressed.

Exodus 20:1-17 King James Version (KJV)
[1] And God spake all these words, saying,
[2] I am the Lord thy God, which have brought thee out of the land of Egypt, out of the house of bondage.
[3] Thou shalt have no other gods before me.

[4] Thou shalt not make unto thee any graven image, or any likeness of any thing that is in heaven above, or that is in the earth beneath, or that is in the water under the earth.

[5] Thou shalt not bow down thyself to them, nor serve them: for I the Lord thy God am a jealous God, visiting the iniquity of the fathers upon the children unto the third and fourth generation of them that hate me;

[6] And shewing mercy unto thousands of them that love me and keep my commandments.

[7] Thou shalt not take the name of the Lord thy God in vain; for the Lord will not hold him guiltless that taketh his name in vain.

[8] Remember the sabbath day, to keep it holy.

[9] Six days shalt thou labour and do all thy work:

[10] But the seventh day is the sabbath of the Lord thy God: in it thou shalt not do any work, thou, nor thy son, nor thy daughter, thy manservant, nor thy maidservant, nor thy cattle, nor thy stranger that is within thy gates:

[11] For in six days the Lord made heaven and earth, the sea and all that in them is and rested the seventh day: wherefore the Lord blessed the sabbath day and hallowed it.

[12] Honour thy father and thy mother: that thy days may be long upon the land which the Lord thy God giveth thee.

[13] Thou shalt not kill.

[14] Thou shalt not commit adultery.

[15] Thou shalt not steal.

[16] Thou shalt not bear false witness against thy neighbour.

[17] Thou shalt not covet thy neighbour's house, thou shalt not covet thy neighbour's wife, nor his manservant, nor his maidservant, nor his ox, nor his ass, nor any thing that is thy neighbour's.

In more modern language:

Exodus 20:1-17 Amplified Bible, Classic Edition (AMPC)

[1] Then God spoke all these words:

[2] I am the Lord your God, Who has brought you out of the land of Egypt, out of the house of bondage.

[3] You shall have no other gods before or besides Me.

[4] You shall not make yourself any graven image [to worship it] or any likeness of anything that is in the heavens above, or that is in the earth beneath, or that is in the water under the earth;

[5] You shall not bow down yourself to them or serve them; for I the Lord your God am a jealous God, visiting the iniquity of the fathers upon the children to the third and fourth generation of those who hate Me,

[6] But showing mercy and steadfast love to a thousand generations of those who love Me and keep My commandments.

[7] You shall not use or repeat the name of the Lord your God in vain [that is, lightly or frivolously, in false affirmations or profanely]; for the Lord will not hold him guiltless who takes His name in vain.

[8] [Earnestly] remember the Sabbath day, to keep it holy (withdrawn from common employment and dedicated to God).

[9] Six days you shall labor and do all your work,

[10] But the seventh day is a Sabbath to the Lord your God; in it you shall not do any work, you, or your son, your daughter, your manservant, your maidservant, your domestic animals, or the sojourner within your gates.

[11] For in six days the Lord made the heavens and the earth, the sea and all that is in them and rested the seventh day. That is why the Lord blessed the Sabbath day and hallowed it [set it apart for His purposes].

[12] Regard (treat with honor, due obedience and courtesy) your father and mother, that your days may be long in the land the Lord your God gives you.

[13] You shall not commit murder.

[14] You shall not commit adultery.

[15] You shall not steal.

[16] You shall not witness falsely against your neighbor.

[17] You shall not covet your neighbor's house, your neighbor's wife, or his manservant, or his maidservant, or his ox, or his donkey, or anything that is your neighbor's.

Lust is about me, myself and I and no one else. We most likely have considered this in the light of sexual sin but it can also be manifested in the way we hoard God's provision for us and us only. In the United States our life style is built around "me first" and "I deserve all that I can get." Hence God's instruction to not partake of the fruit of the tree of the knowledge of good and evil.

Consider how Joseph through the power of the Holy Spirit was able to flee from the sexual advances of Pharaoh's wife. Or consider the parable which Jesus told of the man who had to build extra barns in which to place his crops in for use in his retirement. Or consider the rich young ruler who asked Jesus how to receive eternal life. When he was told he should sell all that he had, give it to the poor, and take up his cross and follow Jesus, the rich young man refused to accept the way out. There are many more examples which you can add to this list. Let's review the steps of temptation which lead to sin.

1. Understand that God is not the source of temptation.

2. It is something that we must first consider in our minds or hearts that leads to something we want or desire. Lust is a part of our character. All of us have lustful desires embedded in us.

3. A temptation is something that must appeal to us and can start as a thought or impression. This thought or idea can come from all sorts of influences such as what we see hear or even taste or smell.

4. The idea can be initiated by Satan, or others or just desires inside of us.

5. We begin to think about the idea at hand and we begin to consider the idea more and more. The more this happens, the more attractive it becomes to us. This can happen consciously or unconsciously.

6. The thought becomes more and more compelling. Finally, when it seems acceptable to us, we perform the act even though we know that the act is wrong to do. Just as Paul said, what he willed to do (the right thing), he didn't do (so he sinned). The law of sin and death wars against the law of righteousness.

Romans 7:14-24 King James Version (KJV)

[14] For we know that the law is spiritual: but I am carnal, sold under sin.

[15] For that which I do I allow not: for what I would, that do I not; but what I hate, that do

[16] If then I do that which I would not, I consent unto the law that it is good.

[17] Now then it is no more I that do it, but sin that dwelleth in me.

[18] For I know that in me (that is, in my flesh,) dwelleth no good thing: for to will is present with me; but how to perform that which is good I find not.

[19] For the good that I would I do not: but the evil which I would not, that I do.

[20] Now if I do that I would not, it is no more I that do it, but sin that dwelleth in me.

[21] I find then a law, that, when I would do good, evil is present with me.

[22] For I delight in the law of God after the inward man:

[23] But I see another law in my members, warring against the law of my mind and bringing me into captivity to the law of sin which is in my members.

[24] O wretched man that I am! who shall deliver me from the body of this death?

Romans 8:1-11 King James Version (KJV)

[1] There is therefore now no condemnation for those who are in Christ Jesus.

[2] For the law of the Spirit of life in Christ Jesus has set you free from the law of sin and of death.

[3] For God has done what the law, weakened by the flesh, could not do: by sending his own Son in the likeness of sinful flesh and to deal with sin, he condemned sin in the flesh,

[4] so that the just requirement of the law might be fulfilled in us, who walk not according to the flesh but according to the Spirit.

[5] For those who live according to the flesh set their minds on the things of the flesh, but those who live according to the Spirit set their minds on the things of the Spirit.

[6] To set the mind on the flesh is death, but to set the mind on the Spirit is life and peace.

[7] For this reason the mind that is set on the flesh is hostile to God; it does not submit to God's law—indeed it cannot,

[8] and those who are in the flesh cannot please God.

[9] But you are not in the flesh; you are in the Spirit, since the Spirit of God dwells in you. Anyone who does not have the Spirit of Christ does not belong to him.

[10] But if Christ is in you, though the body is dead because of sin, the Spirit is life because of righteousness.

[11] If the Spirit of him who raised Jesus from the dead dwells in you, he who raised Christ from the dead will give life to your mortal bodies also through his Spirit that dwells in you.

Luke 10:29 King James Version (KJV)

[29] But he, willing to justify himself, said unto Jesus, And who is my neighbour?

Luke 16:14-16 King James Version (KJV)

[14] And the Pharisees also, who were covetous, heard all these things: and they derided him.

[15] And he said unto them, Ye are they which justify yourselves before men; but God knoweth your hearts: for that which is highly esteemed among men is abomination in the sight of God.

[16] The law and the prophets were until John: since that time the kingdom of God is preached and every man presseth into it.

Romans 12:15-17 King James Version (KJV)

[15] Rejoice with them that do rejoice and weep with them that weep.

[16] Be of the same mind one toward another. Mind not high things, but condescend to men of low estate. Be not wise in your own conceits.

[17] Recompense to no man evil for evil. Provide things honest in the sight of all men.

Proverbs 23:6-8 King James Version (KJV)

[6] Eat thou not the bread of him that hath an evil eye, neither desire thou his dainty meats:

[7] For as he thinketh in his heart, so is he: Eat and drink, saith he to thee; but his heart is not with thee.

[8] The morsel which thou hast eaten shalt thou vomit up and lose thy sweet words.

Look at How Job made covenant with eyes to not look upon a woman to lust after her. God always offers a way to avoid temptation if we choose to take it and by the power of his Holy Spirit we can control the lusts of the flesh.

Job 31:1-4 King James Version (KJV)

[1] I made a covenant with mine eyes; why then should I think upon a maid?

[2] For what portion of God is there from above? and what inheritance of the Almighty from on high?

[3] Is not destruction to the wicked? and a strange punishment to the workers of iniquity?

[4] Doth not he see my ways and count all my steps?

1 Corinthians 10:13 King James Version (KJV)

[13] There hath no temptation taken you but such as is common to man: but God is faithful, who will not suffer you to be tempted above that ye are able; but will with the temptation also make a way to escape, that ye may be able to bear it.

Through study of the scripture by the inspiration of the Holy Spirit we can find many examples of common temptations so that we can be alert to them rearing their ugly heads in our lives. And we can also see how others have either given in to them or avoided them. Consider the following examples.

1. David saw a beautiful woman bathing from his rooftop. He considered her beauty and lust rose up in him. He gave into the

temptation to have sex with her. She was married to another man. David had hundreds of wives and concubines. So why did he need to do this?

2. Joseph fled from Pharaoh's wife, who wanted to have sex with him. God has provided the tools to flee temptation if we wish to put them to use.

1 Corinthians 10:12-14King James Version (KJV)
[12] Wherefore let him that thinketh he standeth take heed lest he fall.
[13] There hath no temptation taken you but such as is common to man: but God is faithful, who will not suffer you to be tempted above that ye are able; but will with the temptation also make a way to escape, that ye may be able to bear it.
[14] Wherefore, my dearly beloved, flee from idolatry.

Through studying, fasting and prayer, aided through the power of the Holy Spirit, we can resist sin. Jesus is our way out of all sin. God promises to change us when we are willing to accept His help in this process. God, through the power of the Holy Spirit, can remove the lusts of the flesh from within us and replace them with His righteousness. As always, this takes place through repentance and our willingness and asking God to perform this work in us.

CHAPTER 18

The Power God Has Provided For Us Through His Spirit

The formula here is:

PG = M X C²

Where

PG = the power of God

M = Man

C² = Christ multiplied by the Comforter (The Holy Spirit)

Early this morning, after having attended the July 2017 CCM Celebration event for a week, the Holy Spirit directed me in prayer. Rather than following my normal routine in this prayer, the Holy Spirit had me thank God for some of His righteous attributes. He began by having me thank God for His compassion and how wonderful it is. Then he had me move on to the next item until I had gone through about ten or so. He had me go through a long list which I will not share here in its entirety, but I will share one more - God's faithfulness. He had me thank Him for His faithfulness. He then led me up through a series of degrees of His faithfulness until He finally led me up to the point where He had me to thank Him for the totality of His faithfulness. It is fully complete with nothing left wanting. God's faithfulness is without loss. There is no dimension of it that is missing anything. It is complete. The same can be said for each of these things which we interpret as the attributes of God:

175

- Faith
- Love
- Patience
- Kindness
- Compassion
- And so many more

In each of these He led me to the final point. In all His ways, He is perfect.

Deuteronomy 32:3-4 King James Version (KJV)
[3] Because I will publish the name of the Lord: ascribe ye greatness unto our God.
[4] He is the Rock, his work is perfect: for all his ways are judgment: a God of truth and without iniquity, just and right is he.

He in every way is perfect. For years I have been reading this, but this day, he finally was able to place it in my spirit so that now I understand this. It is not just someone in the past describing as best he can his experience of the living God, but it is God trying to get across to us, as His people, that this is truly who and what he is.

Now for the other portion of this experience. After the Holy Spirit had taken me through this list, He started turning my attention toward himself. He started by allowing me to know all these same attributes are in Him and since He is resident in us, they are there in us to access. God wants us to duplicate these qualities in our life and through the power of the Holy Spirit, we can have them whenever we desire. It is not something we can do on our own, we need the power placed in the Holy Spirit for this work to occur. No matter how hard we try, we cannot achieve the level of perfection needed for these attributes to be a part of us to the level of perfection which God desires, without the renewing work of the Holy Spirit.

Ezekiel 36:26 King James Version (KJV)
[26] A new heart also will I give you and a new spirit will I put within you: and I will take away the stony heart out of your flesh and I will give you an heart of flesh.

The problem is that most of us do not understand that this aspect of the Holy Sprit's work is just sitting inside of us waiting to be unleashed. When we admit without Him there is nothing we can do, then the Holy Spirit is able to start integrating these attributes into our life, so that we can start walking in the

Spirit as God intends for each of us. This process is painless and delightful. It is the work the Holy Spirit was sent to perform when we are ready for it.

Galatians 5:22-23 King James Version (KJV)
²² But the fruit of the Spirit is love, joy, peace, longsuffering, gentleness, goodness, faith,
²³ Meekness, temperance: against such there is no law.

Scripture tells us we were made in His image, but sin has marred that image so that it does not even closely resemble the original intent. The lusts of the flesh, which are present in all of us, cause us to be at war with the righteousness of God.

Romans 8:1-11 King James Version (KJV)
¹ There is therefore now no condemnation for those who are in Christ Jesus.
² For the law of the Spirit of life in Christ Jesus has set you free from the law of sin and of death.
³ For God has done what the law, weakened by the flesh, could not do: by sending his own Son in the likeness of sinful flesh and to deal with sin, he condemned sin in the flesh,
⁴ so that the just requirement of the law might be fulfilled in us, who walk not according to the flesh but according to the Spirit.
⁵ For those who live according to the flesh set their minds on the things of the flesh, but those who live according to the Spirit set their minds on the things of the Spirit.
⁶ To set the mind on the flesh is death, but to set the mind on the Spirit is life and peace.
⁷ For this reason the mind that is set on the flesh is hostile to God; it does not submit to God's law—indeed it cannot,
⁸ and those who are in the flesh cannot please God.
⁹ But you are not in the flesh; you are in the Spirit, since the Spirit of God dwells in you. Anyone who does not have the Spirit of Christ does not belong to him.
¹⁰ But if Christ is in you, though the body is dead because of sin, the Spirit is life because of righteousness.
¹¹ If the Spirit of him who raised Jesus from the dead dwells in you, he who raised Christ from the dead will give life to your mortal bodies also through his Spirit that dwells in you.

The Holy Spirit can correct this and bring about a transformation in us, which can displace those iniquitous desires and actions and those unrighteous traits in us. We can be transformed to the state where they will be as His are. This is how we can achieve the level of change necessary to be the ones prepared to meet Jesus at His return. It takes the Holy Spirit through our cooperation for this to occur. He has the power to start this transformation only when we are ready to accept it and truly desire for it to happen.

Romans 12:1-3 King James Version (KJV)
[1] I beseech you therefore, brethren, by the mercies of God, that ye present your bodies a living sacrifice, holy, acceptable unto God, which is your reasonable service.
[2] And be not conformed to this world: but be ye transformed by the renewing of your mind, that ye may prove what is that good and acceptable and perfect, will of God.
[3] For I say, through the grace given unto me, to every man that is among you, not to think of himself more highly than he ought to think; but to think soberly, according as God hath dealt to every man the measure of faith.

For some, this can happen in a twinkling of an eye, but others like me, it may take a little longer. God provides a description of this occurring to those on the day of Pentecost. All of a sudden those in the upper room, along with 3,000 others, had a miraculous transformation occur. This occurred after the Holy Spirit was able to teach them all, using the Old Testament scriptures, what He was there to perform. He explained the inner peace and power it would bring into their lives and the lives of those they came in contact with. Then, by the power of God, he was able to become one with them and them one with each other. We have specific examples of this provided by the twelve disciples, Paul and Stephen and others mentioned in the New Testament. We can see this in those like Ananias and Sapphira and many other examples of those who were only coming along with a false representation of the work of the Holy Spirit.

Acts 5:1-11 King James Version (KJV)
[1] But a certain man named Ananias, with Sapphira his wife, sold a possession,
[2] And kept back part of the price, his wife also being privy to it and brought a certain part and laid it at the apostles' feet.
[3] But Peter said, Ananias, why hath Satan filled thine heart to lie to the Holy Ghost and to keep back part of the price of the land?
[4] Whiles it remained, was it not thine own? and after it was sold, was it not in thine own power? why hast thou conceived this thing in thine heart? thou hast not lied unto men, but unto God.
[5] And Ananias hearing these words fell down and gave up the ghost: and great fear came on all them that heard these things.
[6] And the young men arose, wound him up and carried him out and buried him.
[7] And it was about the space of three hours after, when his wife, not knowing what was done, came in.
[8] And Peter answered unto her, Tell me whether ye sold the land for so much? And she said, Yea, for so much.
[9] Then Peter said unto her, How is it that ye have agreed together to tempt the Spirit of the Lord? behold, the feet of them which have buried thy husband are at the door and shall carry thee out.

¹⁰ Then fell she down straightway at his feet and yielded up the ghost: and the young men came in and found her dead and, carrying her forth, buried her by her husband. ¹¹ And great fear came upon all the church and upon as many as heard

The Holy Spirit is that self-same spirit who was the co-participant with God in the creation of heaven and earth. He is that self-same spirit which raised Jesus from the dead and the self-same spirit in which God has shared all power. God has told us through Christ Jesus that if we had the faith the size of a grain of mustard seed that we could move mountains, that we all have a measure of faith and that the same works He did we can do and even more. Why? The Holy Spirit pointed out we have access to all this power through Him after we have allowed him to impart the righteousness of God. All of these attributes of God are there in the Holy Spirit for us, waiting to be released. When we allow this to occur, we can fulfill scripture. We will be able to move mountains and heal the sick and find comfort in the comforter because we have access to all of this through Him. And all of this is so that God may finally bring about His Kingdom on earth.

This power is lying dormant in us because we have made the wrong things the priority in our lives. We have made it a goal to seek fame and fortune and comfort on this earth. We are missing the true comforter. God has told us to seek first His kingdom and His righteousness then all these things will be added unto us, but like the Israelites of old, we have made earthly comfort our primary goal and have placed the work of God in the background.

The Holy Spirit pointed out how we have discovered how to unleash the power of the atom. One of the tiniest of all particles, yet God has placed in it so much power that if released, it can be utterly destructively, or it can be used for good to power our homes. Yet, we still don't have a handle on the most efficient way to harness this energy. The same holds true for the power we have resident in us through the Holy Spirit. Do we not see that the same power that created the Universe is in us so that we have access to unlimited power to bring about the change of our fellow brothers and sisters in love? We have within us the power to be transformed into the likeness of Christ Jesus, the power to bring about His Kingdom on earth, the power to heal the sick, the power to bring peace on earth and oh so much more! Yes! We can move mountains through the power of the Holy Spirit if it is necessary for us to build

The Kingdom. When we allow the Holy Spirit to implant His righteousness in us, we will be able to make decisions the same way God does. We will make right choices and right decisions and become one with God and our fellow saints. Fellow saints, I call on you to fall on your knees and repent so God can heal our nation and our world. Admit that our nature is sinful and that we need to be transformed through the Holy Spirit to be like Him, having had our thoughts, desires and heart converted. We need to give him permission to perform the work of regeneration in us, renewing our body mind and spirit to be what He intended from the beginning.

I end with this. God is searching the earth for those who are willing to accept the task of building His Kingdom here on earth. He is looking for those who are willing to put earthly priorities aside so He can release the Holy Spirit to perform that marvelous work and wonder intended from the beginning that we may be like Him.

Matthew 6:33 King James Version (KJV)
[33] But seek ye first the kingdom of God and his righteousness; and all these things shall be added unto you.

Matthew 17:20 King James Version (KJV)
[20] And Jesus said unto them, Because of your unbelief: for verily I say unto you, If ye have faith as a grain of mustard seed, ye shall say unto this mountain, Remove hence to yonder place; and it shall remove; and nothing shall be impossible unto you.

1 John 3:1-3 King James Version (KJV)
[1] Behold, what manner of love the Father hath bestowed upon us, that we should be called the sons of God: therefore the world knoweth us not, because it knew him not.
[2] Beloved, now are we the sons of God and it doth not yet appear what we shall be: but we know that, when he shall appear, we shall be like him; for we shall see him as he is.
[3] And every man that hath this hope in him purifieth himself, even as he is pure.

Genesis 1:1-3 King James Version (KJV)
[1] In the beginning God created the heaven and the earth.
[2] And the earth was without form and void; and darkness was upon the face of the deep. And the Spirit of God moved upon the face of the waters.

Romans 8:10-12 King James Version (KJV)
[10] And if Christ be in you, the body is dead because of sin; but the Spirit is life because of righteousness.
[11] But if the Spirit of him that raised up Jesus from the dead dwell in you, he that raised up Christ from the dead shall also quicken your mortal bodies by his Spirit that dwelleth in you.
[12] Therefore, brethren, we are debtors, not to the flesh, to live after the flesh.

CHAPTER 19

Conclusion

Scripture is a living breathing entity which requires the illumination of the Holy Spirit. Without Him they are like the dead sea scrolls, torn and incomplete like a puzzle missing pieces. We can't complete it. Just as Jesus spoke in parables to those who were not ready for the illumination of the purposes of God, the bible presents the same image to those who are not led by the Holy Spirit to understand its meaning. This body of work is the same. Without the illumination of the Holy Spirit, this is a dead work to you. Since scripture that is inspired by God is living, when illuminated by the Holy Spirit, it exposes the work of God. Each time we read it, He is able to expand the meaning to us based on our point of conversion and our personal need. It is not that God changes, it is our understanding of God that changes. May God provide His blessing to you for your spiritual growth.

Just because this book is ending at this time, it does not mean there are no more formulas in the Bible? The answer is no. The thing that you should see from this work is that the work of God in man cannot be accomplished without three steps. First, we have to admit that we cannot be the person God wants us to be on our own. Second, we need to turn to Jesus and admit that we have sinned and accept His forgiveness. Third, we must ask for Him and the Holy Spirit to provide the conversion that our spirit is required to undergo and willingly submit to the process.

Scripture References

Lorenzo Hill

Lorenzo Hill has served in the ministry of the Community of Christ (formerly The Reorganized Church Of Jesus Christ Of Latter Day Saints) since 1976 when he was ordained a priest. Throughout his ministry he has been a self-supporting minister. He has served in his current office of Evangelist since 1988 and continues to be very active in ministry, serving in many different roles of leadership and service. Lorenzo was raised in St. Louis Missouri and resided there until he received his Bachelor of Science degree in Chemical Engineering in 1970 from the Missouri School of Science and Technology (formerly the University of Missouri at Rolla). He is a registered professional engineer. He has worked in the petroleum industry since he graduated from college and has retired twice. Needless to say, he has moved around quite a bit. He and his wife of 48 years, Clotilde, have three children, Alicia Renee, Reynada Charlese (husband Courtney) and a son, Jared Lorenzo. Though he has taken many post graduate courses in both engineering and ministry, Lorenzo chose not to pursue an advanced degree. He has written numerous technical reports and technical texts for the training and instruction of engineers and construction inspectors. All of these works, however, were prepared for either clients or for internal company use and as such, were not issued as external publications.

Formulas In The Scripture E=MC^2 is Lorenzo's first public work.